# Fresh Ways
## with Beef & Veal

Time-Life Books Inc.
is a wholly owned subsidiary of
**TIME INCORPORATED**

*Editor-in-Chief:* Jason McManus
*Chairman and Chief Executive Officer:* J. Richard Munro
*President and Chief Operating Officer:* N. J. Nicholas, Jr.
*Editorial Director:* Richard B. Stolley

THE TIME INC. BOOK COMPANY

*President and Chief Executive Officer:* Kelso F. Sutton
*President, Time Inc. Books Direct:* Christopher T. Linen

*COVER*

*A filling of fresh basil and sun-dried tomatoes enlivens this lean, beef tenderloin roast. Accompanied by cherry tomatoes stuffed with a light purée made of yogurt, basil, and garlic, this dish (recipe, pages 50-51), provides a meal that is flavorful and satisfying, yet has only 4 grams of saturated fat and 340 calories.*

## TIME-LIFE BOOKS INC.

EDITOR: George Constable
*Executive Editor:* Ellen Phillips
*Director of Design:* Louis Klein
*Director of Editorial Resources:* Phyllis K. Wise
*Editorial Board:* Russell B. Adams, Jr., Dale M. Brown, Roberta Conlan, Thomas H. Flaherty, Lee Hassig, Donia Ann Steele, Rosalind Stubenberg
*Director of Photography and Research:* John Conrad Weiser
*Assistant Director of Editorial Resources:* Elise Ritter Gibson

EUROPEAN EDITOR: Sue Joiner
*Executive Editor:* Gillian Moore
*Design Director:* Ed Skyner
*Assistant Design Director:* Mary Staples
*Chief of Research:* Vanessa Kramer
*Chief Sub-Editor:* Ilse Gray

PRESIDENT: John M. Fahey, Jr.
*Senior Vice Presidents:* Robert M. DeSena, James L. Mercer, Paul R. Stewart, Joseph J. Ward
*Vice Presidents:* Stephen L. Bair, Stephen L. Goldstein, Juanita T. James, Andrew P. Kaplan, Carol Kaplan, Susan J. Maruyama, Robert H. Smith
*Supervisor of Quality Control:* James King

PUBLISHER: Joseph J. Ward

**Library of Congress Cataloging in Publication Data**
Fresh ways with beef & veal / by the editors of Time-Life Books.
    p.    cm. — (Healthy home cooking)
    Includes index.
    ISBN 0-8094-6087-4. — ISBN 0-8094-6088-2 (lib. bdg.)
    1. Cookery (Beef). 2. Cookery (Veal).
I. Time-Life Books.      II. Title: Fresh ways with beef and veal.
III. Series.
TX749.5.B43F74 1989                           89-4385
641.6'62—dc19                                     CIP

For information on and a full description of any Time-Life Books series, please call 1-800-621-7026 or write:
Reader Information
Time-Life Customer Service
P.O. Box C-32068
Richmond, Virginia 23261-2068

Time-Life Books Inc. offers a wide range of fine recordings, including a *Rock 'n' Roll Era* series. For subscription information, call 1-800-621-7026 or write Time-Life Music, P.O. Box C-32068, Richmond, Virginia 23261-2068.

## HEALTHY HOME COOKING

SERIES DIRECTORS: Dale M. Brown, Jackie Matthews

Editorial Staff for *Fresh Ways with Beef & Veal:*
*Book Manager:* Susan Stuck
*Designer:* Lynne Brown
*Picture Editor:* Sally Collins
*Associate Picture Editor:* Scarlet Cheng
*Text Editor:* Allan Fallow
*Researcher/Writers:* Henry Grossi, Andrea Reynolds
*Sub-Editor:* Wendy Gibbons
*Picture Coordinator:* Linda Yates
*Photographer's Assistant:* Mazyar Parvaresh
*Kitchen Assistant:* Chhomaly Sok

EDITORIAL PRODUCTION:
*Chief:* Maureen Kelly
*Assistant:* Samantha Hill
*Editorial Department:* Theresa John, Debra Lelliott

U.S. Edition:
*Assistant Editor:* Barbara Fairchild Quarmby
*Copy Coordinator:* Anne Farr
*Picture Coordinator:* Betty H. Weatherley

Editorial Operations
*Copy Chief:* Diane Ullius
*Production:* Celia Beattie
*Library:* Louise D. Forstall

Correspondents: Elisabeth Kraemer-Singh (Bonn); Christina Lieberman (New York); Maria Vincenza Aloisi (Paris); Ann Natanson (Rome).

## THE COOKS

PAT ALBUREY is a home economist with a wide experience in preparing foods for photography, teaching cooking, and creating recipes. She has written a number of cookbooks, and she was the studio consultant for the Time-Life Books series The Good Cook. She has created a number of the recipes in this volume.

LISA CHERKASKY has worked as a chef at numerous restaurants in Washington, D.C., and in Madison, Wisconsin, including nationally known Le Pavillon and Le Lion d'Or. A graduate of The Culinary Institute of America at Hyde Park, New York, she has also taught classes in French cooking technique.

ADAM DE VITO began his cooking apprenticeship when he was only 14. He has worked at Le Pavillon restaurant in Washington, D.C., taught with food writer Madeleine Kamman, and conducted classes at L'Académie de Cuisine.

JOHN T. SHAFFER is a graduate of The Culinary Institute of America. He has had broad experience as a chef, including five years at The Four Seasons Hotel in Washington, D.C.

## THE CONSULTANTS

CAROL CUTLER is the author of many cookbooks. During the 12 years she lived in France, she studied at the Cordon Bleu and the École des Trois Gourmandes, as well as with private chefs.

NORMA MACMILLAN has written several cookbooks and edited many others. She has worked on various food publications, including *Grand Diplôme* and *Supercook,* and some of the recipes for this volume were created by her. She lives and works in London.

MARY JO FEENEY, who has a master's degree in nutrition from Case-Western Reserve University, Cleveland, Ohio, is a registered dietitian with 15 years experience in the healthcare field. She is the author of the U.S. consumer information brochure *Light Cooking with Beef* and *California Beef,* a computerized cookbook.

## THE NUTRITION CONSULTANTS

PATRICIA JUDD trained as a dietitian and worked in hospital nutrition before returning to college to earn her M.Sc. and Ph.D. degrees. She has since lectured in Nutrition and Dietetics at London University.

JANET TENNEY has been involved in nutrition and consumer affairs since she received her master's degree in human nutrition from Columbia University.

Nutritional analyses for *Fresh Ways with Beef & Veal* were derived from Practorcare's Nutriplanner System and other current data.

*Other Publications:*

This volume is one of a series of illustrated cookbooks that emphasize the preparation of healthful dishes for today's weight-conscious, nutrition-minded eaters.

# *Fresh Ways with Beef & Veal*

BY

THE EDITORS OF TIME-LIFE BOOKS

TIME-LIFE BOOKS / ALEXANDRIA, VIRGINIA

# Contents

Grilled Top Loin Steaks with Glazed Shallots and Mushrooms

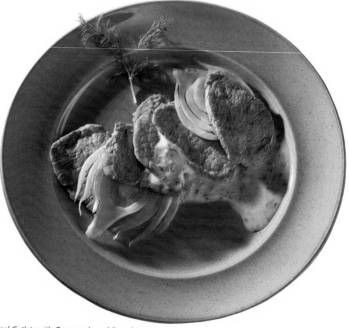

Veal Cutlets with Gorgonzola and Fennel

Veal, Peach, and Peppercorn Pâté

Lime-Ginger Beef

# The New, Lean Beef and Veal

Mention red meat and beef springs to mind, setting mouths to watering with the thought of majestic cuts and robust flavor. So different is the pale flesh and subtle flavor of veal that it scarcely seems possible that these two meats come from the same animal.

What beef and veal share is the real satisfaction that they can offer to diner and cook alike. Both meats lend themselves to a variety of different cooking methods and unite happily with a wide range of other foods. And while beef has long held a central place in the American culinary tradition, veal is rapidly gaining in popularity.

This volume celebrates the old-fashioned virtues of beef and veal; but it does so in a modern way, concentrating on lean cuts cooked in little additional fat and served in healthful 3-ounce portions (each based on 4 ounces of trimmed raw meat). The recipes thus make it possible for lovers of beef and veal to have their meat and address their health concerns too.

book's 3-ounce helpings of cooked, lean beef—which have less than 180 calories—supply 45 percent of the 60 grams of protein that an adult should have in his or her daily diet. Beef also contains many of the nutrients that we need in minute amounts—milligrams or micrograms—in our diet. A 3-ounce portion of cooked beef supplies all of the vitamin $B_{12}$, about 30 percent of the thiamine, and about 20 percent of the niacin an adult male should consume every day. The same portion also provides 25 percent of his daily iron requirement.

Moreover, 40 to 60 percent of the iron in beef is present as part of the hemoglobin molecule, which gives blood its red color. Since this so-called heme iron is readily absorbed by the body, beef has particular importance to women, for whom iron ranks high among the essential minerals. Heme iron is also valuable for its ability to enhance the body's absorption of iron from other foods.

Veal has even fewer calories, a mere 120 calories being present in a cutlet. And, with today's trend toward lean, supertrimmed cuts, veal can have a fat level as low as 5 percent.

In developing the 109 dishes that follow, the Time-Life cooks have heeded recommendations from nutritionists that we cut down on the fat in our diet. Studies have shown that we obtain some 40 percent of our calories from fat and that we would be much better off if we reduced that amount to around 30 percent. As the recipes in this volume will demonstrate, this is a goal that can be met by selecting and preparing lean cuts of beef and veal wisely, without compromising taste and thus curtailing the pleasure both meats offer so abundantly. The cooks have been particularly careful to restrict the amount of saturated fat in their recipes, since it is this type of fat that raises the level of cholesterol in the blood and that is thought to increase the risk of heart disease. Nutritionists recommend that less than 15 percent of our calories come from saturated fat.

Contrary to what most people believe, beef and veal are not overloaded with cholesterol. A 3½-ounce serving of beef, for example, averages 85 milligrams of cholesterol; the same weight of veal averages 90 milligrams of cholesterol. Most other meats and some fish have cholesterol levels comparable with those of beef and veal.

For our dishes, we have chosen beef and veal cuts (charts, page 9) from the least fatty parts of the animals. Yet it is fat, of course, that gives meat, especially red meat, much of its flavor and juiciness. Because we have avoided the fattier cuts, we have employed methods and ingredients that ensure flavor and moistness. And we have been very careful not to overcook the meat—which is easy to do with lean cuts, particularly when pieces are small. Prolonged high heat is the surest way to toughen meat, and to dry it out and shrink it as well.

## The nutritional aspects

Beef and veal are very good for you. They are considered nutrient-dense foods, which means, simply, that a small amount provides a high level of essential nutrients with relatively few calories. This

For roasting, broiling, and grilling beef we recommend that it be cooked rare or medium rare. In large cuts this can be ascertained by inserting a meat thermometer in the thickest part of the meat and letting the temperature reach 140° F. (Such a temperature also guarantees that any harmful organisms that might be present will be killed.) An instant-reading thermometer, which registers temperatures just 10 seconds after insertion, can be very handy, especially when the piece is small. After the desired 140° F. temperature has been reached, let the beef rest away from the heat for up to 15 minutes, during which time its internal temperature will rise five more degrees—just right for medium-rare beef. Veal, however, is most palatable when its juices have lost their pink tinge; although, like beef, it becomes tough when overcooked.

Because the recipes call for very small amounts of cooking oil, we encourage the use of nonstick skillets wherever possible. To further keep down calories and to restrict saturated fat, we make little use of cream, butter, and cheese in sauces, and any fat that may have melted out of the meat is discarded. We obtain smooth, well-flavored sauces by reducing the liquids in which the meat and other ingredients have been simmered, thus retaining their nutrients.

With tougher cuts, we may pound the meat to tenderize it. Some recipes call for carving the meat diagonally across the grain, which produces slices that are easy to chew. Sometimes we cut meat into small pieces or strips so that they can cook quickly. For stir-frying, the raw meat is sliced into thin strips and tossed in a wok or frying pan, then removed and replaced by the vegetables called for in the recipe. Only when the vegetables are ready is the meat returned to the pan and reheated, a measure that keeps it from overcooking and turning leathery. We do not salt the meat before grilling, roasting, or broiling it because salt draws out the juices, producing dry meat.

## Reshaping the animals themselves

Thanks to the meat industry's efforts, beef and veal are leaner than they used to be. Farmers are raising leaner beef breeds: Cattle spend more time eating grass and less time being finished, or fattened, on grain than in the past. Many veal calves are now reared in barns and allowed to move freely. This arrangement not only is more humane than the old system of keeping the calves in confined spaces; it also makes them burn more calories and thus results in a leaner carcass.

As farmers strive for leaner cattle, so retailers aim for leaner cuts, trimming fat to within an eighth of an inch of the flesh. You should buy trimmed meat and trim it again at home.

## Storing beef and veal

Both of these meats are less perishable than poultry and fish. Steaks and larger cuts can be kept for up to four days in a refrigerator set between 35° F. and 43° F. Meat that has been ground or chopped, however, should never be kept longer than two to three days. For storage, meat from the butcher should be unwrapped, set on a plate, loosely covered with wax paper, and then covered with a dish that allows air to circulate, thus eliminating the damp environment that causes bacteria to thrive. Cuts from the supermarket sold in special airtight wrapping can be stored in their wrapping.

Preparing meat for freezing involves wrapping it tightly in tough, moistureproof plastic, aluminum foil, or freezer paper, then squeezing all the air from the package. Air pockets cause freezer burn, which dries out meat and adversely affects its color, texture, and flavor.

Roasts or pieces of meat that have been properly wrapped may be kept in a freezer up to a year in the case of beef and up to six months in the case of veal, providing they are quickly frozen and maintained at 0° F. or lower. Any meat, whether beef or veal, that has been ground or chopped should not be kept longer than three months in the freezer.

## About the book's organization

This book falls into five sections, covering, respectively, grilling, broiling, and roasting; stir-frying and sautéing; moist methods; mixed methods; and, finally, microwaving. In each section, the beef recipes are grouped together, followed by the veal recipes. Most recipes come with suggestions for accompanying vegetables or starches. For generalized techniques common to a number of the recipes, such as stuffing a steak or rolling a paupiette of veal, there are step-by-step instructions.

Dry-heat methods such as grilling and stir-frying are generally applied to steaks, chops, and tender roasts. Moist-heat methods such as braising are reserved mostly for tougher cuts. Vegetables are often cooked with the meat to provide moisture as well as flavor; herbs, spices, fruits and fruit juices, wines, and spirits are called upon to increase the appeal of the dishes, all of which are low in salt. Many of the recipes ask for unsalted brown, veal, or chicken stock (recipes, page 138). A glossary toward the end of the volume identifies and describes ingredients or techniques that may be unfamiliar.

All recipes not only take into account your concerns about fat but also provide information about nutrition in general. Printed beside each recipe is a breakdown of nutrients per single serving—approximate counts for calories, protein, cholesterol, total fat, saturated fat (the kind that increases the body's blood cholesterol), and sodium. This analysis should make it easier for you to plan the rest of your meal—and the other menus for the day as well—so that you can ensure that fewer of the calories you consume come from fat.

## The Key to Better Eating

Healthy Home Cooking addresses the concerns of today's weight-conscious, health-minded cooks with recipes developed within strict nutritional guidelines.

The chart at right presents the National Research Council's Recommended Dietary Allowances of calories and protein for healthy men, women, and children of average size, along with the council's recommendations for the "safe and adequate" maximum intake of sodium. Although the council has not established similar recommendations for either cholesterol or fat, the chart does include what the National Institutes of Health and the American Heart Association consider the maximum allowable amounts of these in one day's eating for healthy members of the general population.

The volumes in this series do not purport to be diet books, nor do they focus on health foods. Rather, the books express a common-sense approach to cooking that uses salt, sugar, cream, butter, and oil in moderation while including other ingredients that contribute flavor and satisfaction as well. The portions themselves are modest in size.

The recipes make few unusual demands. Naturally they call for fresh ingredients, suggesting substitutes should these be unavailable. (Only the original ingredient is calculated in the nutrient analysis, however.) Most of the ingredients can be found in any well-stocked supermarket; the occasional exceptions can be bought in specialty shops or ethnic food stores.

### Recommended Dietary Guidelines

| | | Average Daily Intake | | Maximum Daily Intake | | | |
|---|---|---|---|---|---|---|---|
| | | CALORIES | PROTEIN grams | CHOLESTEROL milligrams | TOTAL FAT grams | SATURATED FAT grams | SODIUM milligrams |
| Children | 7-10 | 2400 | 22 | 240 | 80 | 27 | 1800 |
| Females | 11-14 | 2200 | 37 | 220 | 73 | 24 | 2700 |
| | 15-18 | 2100 | 44 | 210 | 70 | 23 | 2700 |
| | 19-22 | 2100 | 44 | 300 | 70 | 23 | 3300 |
| | 23-50 | 2000 | 44 | 300 | 67 | 22 | 3300 |
| | 51-75 | 1800 | 44 | 300 | 60 | 20 | 3300 |
| Males | 11-14 | 2700 | 36 | 270 | 90 | 30 | 2700 |
| | 15-18 | 2800 | 56 | 280 | 93 | 31 | 2700 |
| | 19-22 | 2900 | 56 | 300 | 97 | 32 | 3300 |
| | 23-50 | 2700 | 56 | 300 | 90 | 30 | 3300 |
| | 51-75 | 2400 | 56 | 300 | 80 | 27 | 3300 |

### About cooking times

To help the cook plan ahead effectively, Healthy Home Cooking takes time into account in all its recipes. While recognizing that everyone cooks at a different speed and that stoves and ovens may differ somewhat in their temperatures, the series provides approximate "working" and "total" times for every dish. Working time stands for the minutes actively spent on preparation; total time includes unattended cooking time, as well as time devoted to marinating, soaking, cooling, or chilling various ingredients. Because the recipes emphasize fresh foods, the dishes may take a bit longer to prepare than those in "quick and easy" cookbooks that call for canned or packaged products, but the difference in flavor, and often in added nutritional value, should compensate for the little extra time involved.

### Chilies—A Cautionary Note

Both dried and fresh hot chilies should be handled with care; their flesh and seeds contain volatile oils that can make skin tingle and cause eyes to burn. Rubber gloves offer protection—but the cook should still be careful not to touch the face, lips, or eyes when working with chilies.

Soaking fresh chilies in cold, salted water for an hour will remove some of their fire. If canned chilies are substituted for fresh ones, they should be rinsed in cold water in order to eliminate as much of the brine used to preserve them as possible.

## The Leanest of the Lean

These charts show and identify the beef and veal cuts *(colored areas)* that are used in this book. No cut derives more than 45 percent of its calories from fat, and many come in well under that amount.

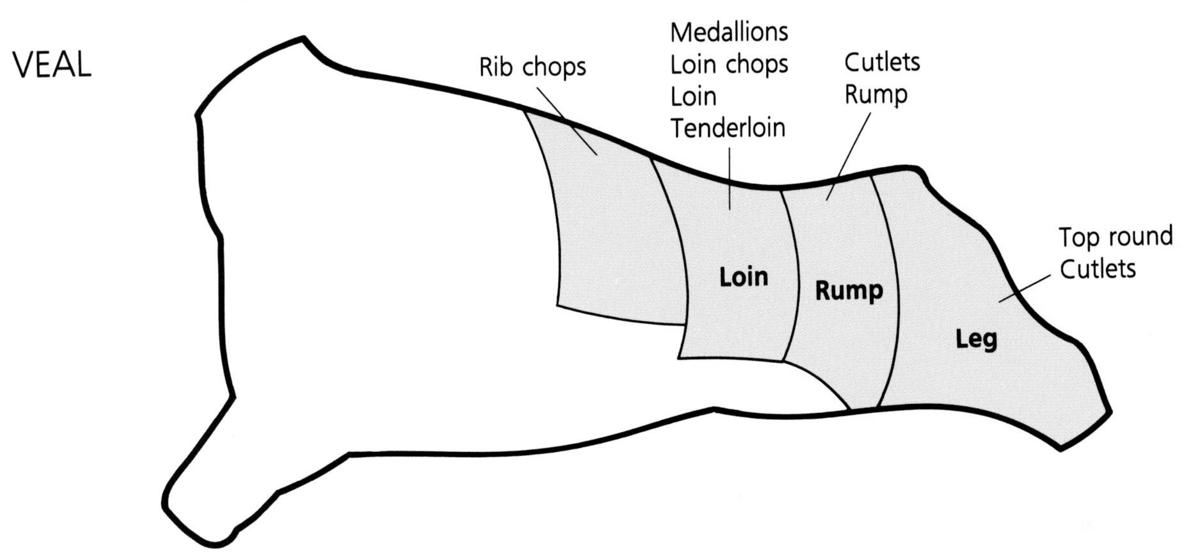

### VEAL

Rib chops

Medallions
Loin chops
Loin
Tenderloin

Cutlets
Rump

Top round
Cutlets

**Loin** **Rump** **Leg**

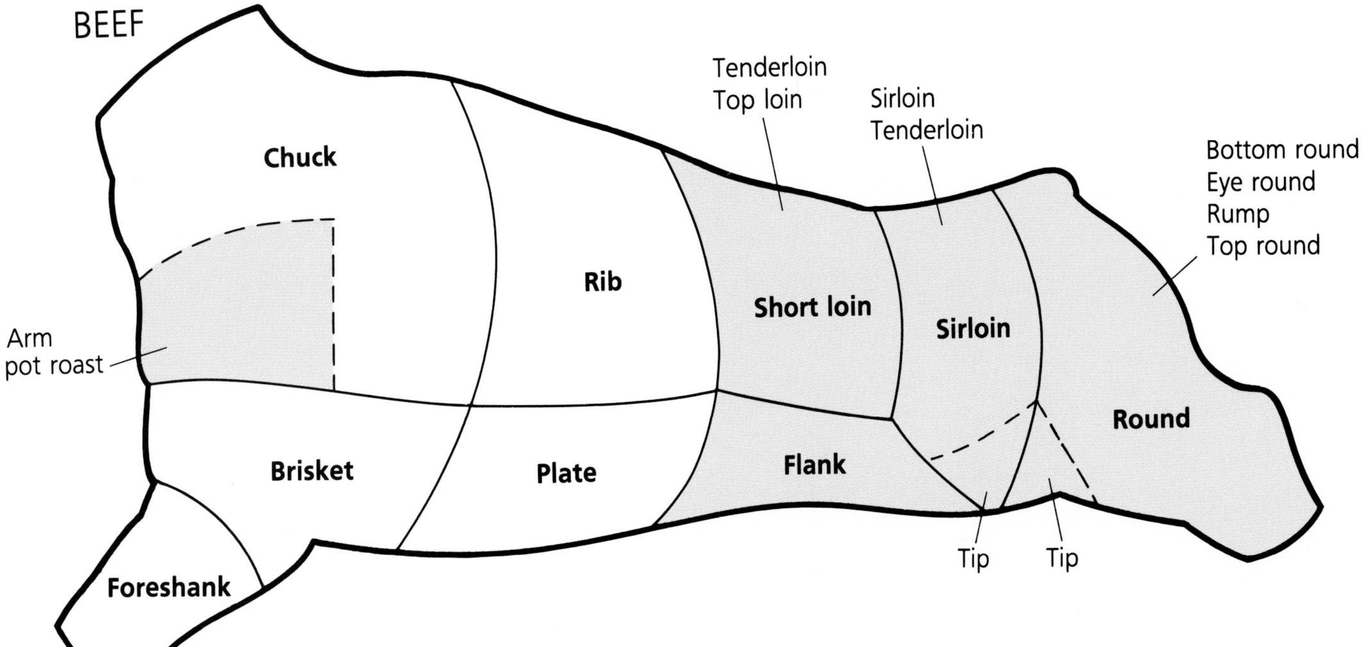

### BEEF

**Chuck**

Tenderloin
Top loin

Sirloin
Tenderloin

Bottom round
Eye round
Rump
Top round

Arm
pot roast

**Rib**

**Short loin**

**Sirloin**

**Round**

**Brisket** **Plate** **Flank**

Tip  Tip

**Foreshank**

*1* *Spread with an aromatic blend of garlic, herbs, and mustard, a lean, boned loin of veal lies ready to be tied and roasted (recipe, page 54).*

# Techniques for Tender Cuts

The first cuts of beef and veal ever to be cooked were probably suspended over an open fire. Present-day roasting, broiling, and grilling have much in common with that ancient technique in that they involve direct dry heat. Roasting employs the all-around heat of a modern oven, whereas broiling or grilling directs heat to only one side of the food at a time—either from above or from below. When beef and veal are subjected to this dry, potentially scorching heat, the chief concern of the cook is to prevent the flesh from drying out. The solution adopted by previous generations of cooks was to use fat in its many guises. Marbling in the muscle itself kept meat moist, as did lardons of pork fat threaded into the meat, bards of fat tied around it, and oil and butter spread liberally over the roast and used to baste it.

Today, however, the health-conscious are concerned about cutting down on fat in all its forms. Marbling varies from cut to cut, and this chapter has rejected fatty rib cuts that used to rank among the most popular cuts for roasting. Instead, we have generally selected beef sirloin or round, and loin of veal. Ground beef is taken from the round and is trimmed of all visible fat before being ground.

Fat for larding, barding, and basting has also been drastically reduced. To compensate for the lack of added fat, vegetable stuffings are often used here to baste beef from within by gradually releasing their natural moisture during cooking.

In the grilled sirloin stuffed with summer vegetables *(page 24)*, for example, a stuffing of green and red peppers combined with zucchini contributes moisture as well as flavor and color. Again, on page 37, watercress, spinach, and walnuts form a pinwheel pattern inside pink roulades of rare beef. When plain roast beef is the order of the day, a modern roasting bag provides one solution, protecting a sirloin from the intense heat of the oven while saving diners from unwanted calories *(page 39)*.

The lean, delicate flesh of veal is saved from drying out by the imaginative use of oil-free marinades and coatings, all of them reflecting veal's ability to merge with a diverse range of flavorings. For example, in veal and apricot brochettes *tikka*-style *(page 36)*, a marinade that includes yogurt, ginger, lime, and a catalog of spices both tenderizes the meat and flavors it. On a distinctly pungent note, a paste of crushed green and black peppercorns provides a protective coating for a loin of veal *(page 55)*. And on page 54, a boned loin of veal receives masterly low-calorie treatment—flavorings of grapefruit and herbs, and frequent bastings with stock.

## Grilled Sirloin Steak with Peach Piccalilli

Serves 6
Working time: about 20 minutes
Total time: about 45 minutes

Calories **205**
Protein **24g.**
Cholesterol **66mg.**
Total fat **7g.**
Saturated fat **3g.**
Sodium **185mg.**

| |
| --- |
| one 1¾-lb. boneless sirloin steak, about 1 inch thick, trimmed of fat |
| 2 tsp. chopped fresh ginger |
| ⅛ tsp. cayenne pepper |
| ¼ tsp. salt |
| **Peach piccalilli** |
| 1 white onion (about ½ lb.) |
| 2 large ripe peaches (about ¾ lb.) |
| ½ tbsp. safflower oil |
| 1 tsp. chopped fresh ginger |
| ⅛ tsp. cayenne pepper |
| 3 tbsp. red wine vinegar |
| ⅛ tsp. salt |
| ¼ cup fresh orange juice |
| 1½ tbsp. chopped cilantro or fresh parsley |

To make the piccalilli, slice the onion in half lengthwise. Cutting with the grain, slice each onion half into strips about ¼ inch wide. Blanch the peaches in boiling water for 30 seconds, then remove them with a slotted spoon. When the peaches are cool enough to handle, peel and pit them; cut the peaches into thin slices.

Heat the oil in a large, nonstick skillet over medium-low heat. Add the onion, ginger, and cayenne pepper and cook the onion until it is translucent—7 to 10 minutes. Stir in the vinegar and salt, then cook the mixture for one minute more. Add the peaches and orange juice. Cook the piccalilli slowly, until the peaches are soft but not mushy—an additional 12 to 15 minutes. Remove the skillet from the heat, and stir in the cilantro or parsley.

If you plan to grill the steak, prepare the coals about 30 minutes before cooking time; to broil, preheat the broiler for 10 minutes. Using your hands, rub the ginger and cayenne pepper into both sides of the steak, and allow it to stand at room temperature until you are ready to cook it.

Cook the steak on the first side for six minutes, then turn it and sprinkle it with the salt. Grill the steak on the second side for five to six minutes for medium-rare meat. Transfer the steak to a platter and let it rest for about five minutes before carving it into thin slices. Serve the peach piccalilli on the side.

SUGGESTED ACCOMPANIMENTS: *sugar snap peas; wild rice.*

# Beef Salad with Carrots and Mint

Serves 6
Working time: about 40 minutes
Total time: about 3 hours (includes marinating)

Calories **255**
Protein **25g.**
Cholesterol **63mg.**
Total fat **11g.**
Saturated fat **3g.**
Sodium **340mg.**

| |
|---|
| one 1¾-lb. top round steak, trimmed of fat |
| ¼ cup unsalted brown stock or unsalted chicken stock (recipes, page 138) |
| 1½ tbsp. low-sodium soy sauce |
| ¼ cup fresh lime juice |
| 2 garlic cloves, finely chopped |
| 2 tsp. sugar |
| freshly ground black pepper |
| 2 tsp. chili paste, or ½ tsp. hot red-pepper flakes |
| 2 tbsp. chopped fresh mint, or 2 tsp. dried mint |
| 3 carrots |
| 1 cucumber, preferably unwaxed, thinly sliced |
| 1 sweet white onion, thinly sliced |
| 6 cherry tomatoes, halved |
| 2 cups shredded daikon radish or regular radish |
| 2 tbsp. safflower oil |

Place the steak in a nonreactive baking dish. In a small bowl, combine the stock, soy sauce, 2 tablespoons of the lime juice, the garlic, sugar, some black pepper, the chili paste or pepper flakes, and half of the mint. Pour this mixture over the steak and let it marinate at room temperature for two hours.

With a channel knife or a paring knife, cut several shallow, lengthwise grooves in each carrot. Thinly slice the carrots and place the resulting flowers in a large bowl. Add the cucumber, onion, tomatoes, and radish to the bowl with the carrots.

Remove the steak from the marinade and pat it dry with paper towels. Strain the marinade into a small, nonreactive saucepan and bring it to a boil. Remove the pan from the heat, whisk in the oil and the remaining 2 tablespoons of lime juice, and pour the dressing over the vegetables. Add the rest of the mint and toss well. Set the vegetables aside.

Broil the steak about 3 inches below a preheated broiler until it is medium rare—five to seven minutes per side. Transfer the steak to a cutting board and let it rest for 10 minutes, then slice it against the grain into thin pieces.

Using a slotted spoon, transfer the vegetables to a serving dish. Arrange the steak slices on top of the vegetables; pour the dressing left in the bowl over all, and serve at once.

SUGGESTED ACCOMPANIMENT: *poppy-seed rolls.*

## Grilled Top Loin Steaks with Glazed Shallots and Mushrooms

Serves 4
Working time: about 20 minutes
Total time: about 40 minutes

Calories **290**
Protein **26g.**
Cholesterol **61mg.**
Total fat **9g.**
Saturated fat **3g.**
Sodium **210mg.**

| |
|---|
| 2 top loin steaks (about 10 oz. each), trimmed of fat and cut into 2 pieces |
| 2 tsp. safflower oil |
| ½ lb. mushrooms, wiped clean, halved if large |
| ½ lb. shallots, peeled |
| 2 tbsp. honey |
| 1 tsp. chopped fresh tarragon, or ½ tsp. dried tarragon |
| ½ cup Madeira or port |
| ½ cup unsalted brown stock or unsalted chicken stock (recipes, page 138) |
| 2 tsp. cornstarch mixed with 1 tbsp. of the stock |
| ¼ tsp. salt |
| freshly ground black pepper |

If you plan to grill the steaks, prepare the coals about 30 minutes before cooking time; to broil, preheat the broiler for 10 minutes.

Heat the safflower oil in a nonstick skillet over me-dium heat; add the mushrooms and sauté them until they are lightly browned—about four minutes. Using a slotted spoon, transfer the mushrooms to a bowl. Pour 1 cup of water into the skillet and add the shallots, honey, and tarragon. Partially cover the skillet; bring the liquid to a simmer and cook the mixture until the shallots are translucent and only ¼ cup of liquid remains—8 to 10 minutes.

Return the mushrooms to the skillet and toss them with the shallots and the liquid until all are coated with a syrupy glaze—about two minutes longer. Keep the glazed shallots and mushrooms warm.

In a small, nonreactive saucepan, reduce the Ma-deira or port by half over medium-high heat. Add the stock and bring the mixture to a simmer. Whisk the cornstarch mixture into the simmering liquid. Contin-ue cooking the sauce until it thickens, and add ⅛ teaspoon of the salt and some pepper. Keep the sauce warm while you prepare the steaks.

Cook the steaks for three minutes on the first side. Turn the steaks over and season them with the remaining ⅛ teaspoon of salt and some more pepper. Cook the steaks for three minutes longer for medium-rare meat. Serve the steaks with the glazed shallots and mushrooms on the side and the sauce poured on top.

SUGGESTED ACCOMPANIMENT: *steamed green beans.*

# Low-Fat Hamburgers with Spicy Pumpkin Ketchup

THE RECIPE FOR PUMPKIN KETCHUP YIELDS MORE THAN ENOUGH FOR EIGHT HAMBURGERS; THE EXCESS MAY BE STORED IN THE REFRIGERATOR FOR A WEEK.

Calories **275**
Protein **21g.**
Cholesterol **47mg.**
Total fat **5g.**
Saturated fat **2g.**
Sodium **155mg.**

Serves 8
Working time: about 15 minutes
Total time: about 1 hour and 15 minutes

| |
|---|
| 1¾ lb. beef round, trimmed of fat and ground or chopped (technique, left) |
| 1⅓ cups bulgur |
| 2 garlic cloves, very finely chopped |
| ⅓ cup finely chopped fresh parsley |
| 2 tbsp. grainy mustard |
| **Spicy pumpkin ketchup** |
| 16 oz. canned pumpkin (1½ cups) |
| 1 onion, finely chopped |
| 1 apple or pear, peeled, cored, and chopped |
| ½ cup cider vinegar |
| 2 tbsp. sugar |
| 1 tbsp. honey |
| ½ tsp. ground cloves |
| ½ tsp. curry powder |
| ¼ tsp. ground allspice |
| ¼ tsp. cayenne pepper |
| ¼ tsp. salt |
| freshly ground black pepper |

Combine the ketchup ingredients in a nonreactive saucepan. Stir in 1 cup of water and simmer the mixture over medium-low heat for one hour. Purée the ketchup in a food processor or a blender, then press it through a sieve with a wooden spoon. Transfer the ketchup to a serving bowl and set it aside.

While the ketchup is simmering, put the bulgur into a flameproof bowl and pour 1⅔ cups of boiling water over it. Cover the bowl and set it aside for 30 minutes. ▶

## Guaranteeing Lean Ground Meat Every Time

**Beef and veal bought already ground is often fatty. Even what is labeled "lean" may not be as low in fat as you would like. There is a way, however, to guarantee a lean product—buy a lean cut and ask the butcher to trim and grind it for you. Or you can prepare it at home—either by hand, or using a meat grinder or a food processor. Because none of their juices have been pressed out, hamburgers are particularly delicious when made with hand-chopped beef.**

**1** *SLICING THE MEAT. Trim off all the traces of fat and membrane from the meat—here a piece of top round—and cut the meat into uniform slices. Place the slices on top of one another and cut through to make evenly sized strips.*

**2** *CUBING. Cut the strips of lean meat into fairly small cubes. The chopping will proceed more swiftly if you start with the meat in pieces of roughly equal size.*

**3** *CHOPPING. Spread the meat out on a chopping board and chop it with a matched pair of sharp, heavy knives. With a loose-wristed action, work the knives alternately and rhythmically, as if beating a drum (above, left). As the chopping progresses, the meat will begin to spread out. Stop from time to time and use one of the knives to flip the chopped mass back into the center (above, right): This helps achieve an even texture. Continue chopping until the meat is chopped as coarsely or finely as the recipe dictates.*

If you plan to grill the hamburgers, prepare the coals about 30 minutes before cooking time; to broil, pre-heat the broiler for 10 minutes.

Put the ground beef, soaked bulgur, garlic, parsley, and mustard into a bowl, and combine them thoroughly by hand. Form the mixture into eight patties. Grill or broil the hamburgers for three to four minutes on each side for medium-rare meat. Serve the hamburgers hot with the ketchup alongside.

SUGGESTED ACCOMPANIMENTS: *poppy-seed rolls; sliced tomatoes; lettuce leaves.*

# Sirloin Grilled in Garlic Smoke

Serves 6
Working time: about 30 minutes
Total time: about 45 minutes

Calories **220**
Protein **26g.**
Cholesterol **76mg.**
Total fat **11g.**
Saturated fat **3g.**
Sodium **105mg.**

| |
|---|
| one 2-lb. boneless sirloin steak, about 1½ inches thick, trimmed of fat |
| 10 unpeeled garlic cloves, crushed |
| **Onion-pepper relish** |
| 2 tbsp. safflower oil |
| 1 small red onion, thinly sliced |
| 1 garlic clove, finely chopped |
| 1 tsp. finely chopped fresh ginger |
| 1 sweet green pepper, seeded, deribbed, and julienned |
| 2 scallions, trimmed and thinly sliced |
| 2 tbsp. rice vinegar or distilled white vinegar |
| ¼ tsp. sugar |
| ⅛ tsp. salt |

About 30 minutes before cooking time, prepare the coals in an outdoor grill. Place the crushed garlic cloves in 1 cup of cold water and let them soak while you make the relish.

Heat the oil in a heavy-bottomed or nonstick skillet over medium heat. Add the red-onion slices and cook them, stirring frequently, until they have softened without losing their color—three to four minutes. Add the chopped garlic and ginger, and cook the mixture for 30 seconds longer; transfer it to a bowl. Add the green pepper, scallions, vinegar, sugar, and salt; stir the relish and set it aside.

When the coals are hot, grill the steak for seven minutes on the first side. Drain the water from the garlic cloves. Remove the steak from the grill and toss the soaked garlic cloves directly onto the coals; a garlicky smoke will curl up. Return the steak to the grill and cook it on the second side for five to seven minutes longer for medium-rare meat.

Transfer the steak to a platter and let it rest for five minutes. Carve the steak into thin slices; spread the onion-pepper relish over each portion just before serving, or present the relish on the side.

SUGGESTED ACCOMPANIMENT: *baked potatoes.*

## Grilled Top Loin Steaks with Fennel-Scented Vegetables

Serves 8
Working time: about 20 minutes
Total time: about 40 minutes

| | |
|---|---|
| Calories **235**<br>Protein **26g.**<br>Cholesterol **65mg.**<br>Total fat **10g.**<br>Saturated fat **39g.**<br>Sodium **200mg.** | *4 top loin steaks (about 10 oz. each),*<br>*trimmed of fat* |
| | *2 tbsp. virgin olive oil* |
| | *1½ tsp. fennel seeds, lightly crushed* |
| | *3 garlic cloves, very thinly sliced* |
| | *1 lb. eggplant, cut into ½-inch cubes* |
| | *1 cup chopped onion* |
| | *2 tbsp. fresh lemon juice* |
| | *1½ lb. ripe tomatoes, peeled, seeded,*<br>*and cut into ½-inch pieces* |
| | *½ tsp. salt* |
| | *freshly ground black pepper* |

If you plan to grill the steaks, prepare the coals in an outdoor grill about 30 minutes before cooking time;

to broil, preheat the broiler for about 10 minutes.

In the meantime, heat the olive oil in a large, heavy-bottomed, nonreactive skillet over high heat. When the oil is hot, add the fennel seeds and garlic, and cook them for 30 seconds, stirring constantly. Add the cubed eggplant, onion, and lemon juice, and cook the vegetables for five minutes, stirring frequently. Next, add the tomatoes, ¼ teaspoon of the salt, and a generous grinding of black pepper. Cook the vegetable mixture for three or four minutes longer, stirring continuously. Cover the skillet and set the mixture aside while you finish preparing the dish.

Grill or broil the steaks for three to four minutes on the first side. Turn the steaks over, and sprinkle them with the remaining ¼ teaspoon of salt and some pepper. Cook the steaks for an additional three to four minutes for medium-rare meat. Let the steaks stand for five minutes before thinly slicing them against the grain. Divide the meat and vegetables among eight dinner plates and serve at once.

SUGGESTED ACCOMPANIMENT: *steamed red potatoes.*

## Grilled Roulades with Onion Compote

Serves 4
Working time: about 45 minutes
Total time: about 1 hour

Calories **230**
Protein **21g.**
Cholesterol **44mg.**
Total fat **5g.**
Saturated fat **2g.**
Sodium **305mg.**

| |
| --- |
| *4 eye round steaks (about 1 lb.), trimmed of fat* |
| *1¼ lb. white boiling onions, blanched in boiling water for five minutes, drained, and peeled* |
| *½ cup golden raisins* |
| *⅛ tsp. salt* |
| *1 tsp. red wine vinegar* |
| *¼ cup grainy mustard* |
| *¼ cup finely chopped fresh parsley* |
| *freshly ground black pepper* |

Put the onions, raisins, salt, vinegar, and 1 cup of water into a heavy-bottomed, nonreactive saucepan. Bring the liquid to a boil, then reduce the heat and simmer the mixture until the onions are golden brown and the liquid has evaporated—15 to 20 minutes.

If you plan to grill the roulades, prepare the coals about 30 minutes before cooking time; to broil, preheat the broiler for about 10 minutes.

While the onion compote is simmering, butterfly and pound the steaks as shown opposite. Mix the mustard, parsley, and some pepper in a small bowl, and spread this mixture over the meat. Roll each steak into a loose bundle; tie the roulades with butcher's twine to hold them together.

When the onions finish cooking, set them aside and keep them warm.

Grill or broil the roulades for a total of eight minutes, turning them every two minutes. Transfer the rolls to a platter; serve the onion compote alongside.

SUGGESTED ACCOMPANIMENT: *steamed Brussels sprouts.*

## Butterflying and Pounding a Steak

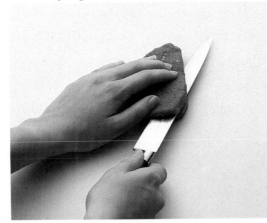

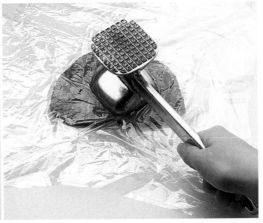

**1** BUTTERFLYING A STEAK. Place the steak flat on a work surface and steady it by pressing it down with one hand. With your other hand, use a thin-bladed knife (here, a slicer) to halve the steak horizontally, stopping just short of the edge so that the two halves remain attached, like the wings of a butterfly.

**2** POUNDING THE MEAT. Unfold the steak and place it on a square of plastic wrap. Cover it with another piece of wrap. Using the smooth end of a meat mallet or the flat of a large, heavy knife, pound the meat to the thickness called for by the recipe.

## Grilled Beef Tenderloin Steaks with Roasted Garlic Sauce

Serves 4
Working time: about 30 minutes
Total time: about 50 minutes

Calories **170**
Protein **20g.**
Cholesterol **55mg.**
Total fat **6g.**
Saturated fat **2g.**
Sodium **100mg.**

| |
|---|
| four 4-oz. beef tenderloin steaks |
| 2 whole garlic bulbs, cloves separated but not peeled |
| ½ tsp. juniper berries, crushed |
| 1 tsp. cracked black peppercorns |
| 1 cup red wine |
| 3 shallots, sliced, or ½ small onion, finely chopped |
| 2 cups unsalted brown stock or unsalted chicken stock (recipes, page 138) |

Preheat the oven to 500° F.

Scatter the garlic cloves in a small baking dish and roast them until they are very soft—20 to 30 minutes. Set the garlic cloves aside to cool.

If you plan to grill the steaks, prepare the coals about 30 minutes before cooking time; to broil, preheat the broiler for about 10 minutes.

In a small bowl, mix together the juniper berries and peppercorns. Press the mixture into both sides of each of the steaks and set them aside at room temperature.

Pour the wine into a small, nonreactive saucepan, and add the shallots or onion. Boil the mixture over medium-high heat until nearly all of the liquid has evaporated—about five minutes. Add the stock, bring the liquid to a boil, and continue cooking it until it is reduced to about 1 cup—approximately five minutes.

Squeeze the garlic pulp from the skins into a food processor or a blender. Pour in the stock and purée the garlic. Put the garlic sauce (it will be thick) into the saucepan and keep it warm.

Cook the steaks for approximately three minutes on each side for medium-rare meat. Serve the steaks with the garlic sauce.

SUGGESTED ACCOMPANIMENT: *oven-fried potatoes.*

# South Seas Kabobs

Serves 4
Working time: about 35 minutes
Total time: about 2 hours and 30 minutes
(includes marinating)

| | |
|---|---|
| Calories **180** | 1 lb. eye round, trimmed of fat |
| Protein **19g.** | and cut into ¾-inch cubes |
| Cholesterol **44mg.** | 1 ripe papaya, peeled, seeded, and cut into 1-inch cubes |
| Total fat **4g.** | 1 sweet red or green pepper, seeded, deribbed, |
| Saturated fat **2g.** | and cut into ¾-inch squares |
| Sodium **195mg.** | |

**Honey-ginger glaze**

¾ cup unsalted brown stock or unsalted chicken stock
(recipes, page 138)

1 scallion, trimmed and thinly sliced

2 garlic cloves, finely chopped

2 tbsp. finely chopped fresh ginger

1 tbsp. honey

¼ tsp. salt

¼ tsp. cracked black peppercorns

1 tbsp. cornstarch, mixed with 1 tbsp. water

Purée about one-third of the papaya in a food processor or a blender; set the remaining cubes aside. Mix

the beef and the papaya purée in a shallow dish; cover
the dish and marinate the beef in the refrigerator for
about two hours.

If you plan to grill the kabobs, prepare the coals
about 30 minutes before cooking time. To broil, preheat the broiler for 10 minutes.

To prepare the glaze, combine the stock, scallion,
garlic, ginger, honey, salt, and cracked peppercorns in
a small saucepan over medium heat. Bring the mixture
to a simmer and cook it for three to four minutes. Stir
in the cornstarch mixture and continue cooking and
stirring the glaze until it thickens—one to two minutes.
Remove the glaze from the heat and set it aside.

To assemble the kabobs, thread the cubes of beef,
papaya, and pepper onto four 12-inch metal skewers.
Cook the kabobs for three minutes. Turn them and
cook them for three minutes more. Brush some glaze
over the kabobs and cook them for one minute. Turn
the kabobs once more, brush them with the glaze, and
cook them for another minute. Transfer the kabobs to
a serving platter and brush them with the remaining
glaze; serve the kabobs immediately.

SUGGESTED ACCOMPANIMENT: *saffron rice tossed with peas.*

# Marinated Beef Salad with Potatoes and Green Beans

Serves 4
Working time: about 25 minutes
Total time: about 3 hours (includes marinating)

Calories **295**
Protein **29g.**
Cholesterol **76mg.**
Total fat **11g.**
Saturated fat **3g.**
Sodium **150mg.**

|  |
|---|
| one 1¼-lb. boneless sirloin steak, about 1-inch thick, trimmed of fat |
| 1 small onion, thinly sliced |
| 1 garlic clove, finely chopped |
| ½ sweet green pepper, finely chopped |
| ⅛ tsp. cracked black peppercorns |
| 1 tbsp. chopped fresh tarragon, or 1 tsp. dried tarragon |
| juice of 2 lemons |
| ½ lb. boiling potatoes, scrubbed and cut into 1-inch cubes |
| ¾ lb. green beans, trimmed |
| ⅛ tsp. salt |
| 1 ripe tomato, cut into wedges |
| 4 tsp. safflower oil |
| 1 tsp. Dijon mustard |

Combine the onion, garlic, green pepper, peppercorns, and tarragon. Scatter half of the mixture on the bottom of a nonreactive pan. Place the steak in the pan and sprinkle the rest of the mixture on top. Pour the lemon juice over the steak, and let it marinate for two hours at room temperature or overnight in the refrigerator.

Cook the potatoes in a saucepan of boiling water until they are tender—7 to 10 minutes. Drain them and set them aside to cool. Pour enough water into the saucepan to fill it to a depth of 1 inch. Set a steamer in the pan and bring the water to a boil over medium-high heat. Add the green beans to the steamer, cover the pan, and steam the beans until they are just tender—about five minutes. Refresh the beans under cold running water, drain them well, and put them into a large salad bowl.

Preheat the broiler for 10 minutes. Remove the steak from the marinade and pour the marinade into a small, nonreactive saucepan. Scrape any clinging marinade ingredients off the steak into the saucepan. Bring the liquid to a boil and simmer it for two minutes. Set it aside until it is needed.

Pat the steak dry with paper towels and broil it for four minutes on the first side. Sprinkle the steak with the salt, turn the steak over, and broil it about four minutes longer for medium-rare meat.

Let the steak rest at room temperature for 30 minutes, then slice it into thin strips. Cut each strip into 2-inch lengths. Add the beef, the cooled potatoes, and the tomatoes to the beans.

Strain the marinade into a small bowl, discarding the solids left in the sieve. Whisk the oil and the mustard into the bowl to make a vinaigrette. Pour the vinaigrette over the salad and toss well. Refrigerate the salad for 20 minutes before serving it.

## Grilled Beef and Fresh Salsa in Flour Tortillas

Serves 4
Working (and total) time: about 1 hour

Calories **375**
Protein **27g.**
Cholesterol **61mg.**
Total fat **10g.**
Saturated fat **2g.**
Sodium **185mg.**

| |
| --- |
| 1 lb. bottom round steak, trimmed of fat |
| 2 tbsp. fresh lime juice |
| 2 tbsp. tequila or gin |
| ½ tsp. chili powder |
| ½ tsp. dried oregano |
| ¼ tsp. ground cumin |
| freshly ground black pepper |
| 8 scallions, the green tops trimmed to 3 inches in length |
| 8 flour tortillas, 10 inches in diameter |
| 2 cups shredded romaine lettuce |

| Salsa |
| --- |
| 1 lb. ripe tomatoes, preferably plum tomatoes, peeled, seeded, and finely chopped |
| 1 sweet green pepper, seeded, deribbed, and finely diced |
| 1 small onion, finely chopped |
| 1 to 3 jalapeño peppers, seeded and finely chopped (cautionary note, page 8) |
| 2 tbsp. fresh lime juice |
| 2 tbsp. chopped cilantro |
| ¼ tsp. salt |

Slice the steak against the grain into ½-inch-wide strips. In a large, shallow, nonreactive dish, combine the lime juice, tequila or gin, chili powder, oregano, cumin, and black pepper. Add the steak strips and the scallions, and toss them well. Let the steak and scallions marinate at room temperature for 20 minutes.

Combine the salsa ingredients in a bowl; let the

salsa stand for at least 15 minutes to blend the flavors.

If you plan to grill the meat, prepare the coals in an outdoor grill about 30 minutes before cooking time; to broil, preheat the broiler for about 10 minutes.

Stack the tortillas and wrap them in aluminum foil. Warm the tortillas in a preheated 350° F. oven for 10 minutes. Meanwhile, cook the steak strips in the center of the grill or broiler, with the scallions laid carefully at the side, for one minute per side; the steak should be medium rare and the scallions lightly charred. Cut the steak strips into pieces about 1 inch long.

To serve, divide the steak pieces and their juices equally among the tortillas. Add some shredded lettuce and a scallion to each tortilla, then spoon some of the salsa over the top. Roll up the tortillas and serve

them at once; pass any remaining salsa separately.

SUGGESTED ACCOMPANIMENT: *black beans and rice.*

EDITOR'S NOTE: *To make flour tortillas, if ready-made ones are unavailable, rub 3 ounces of solid vegetable shortening into 14 ounces of unbleached all-purpose flour mixed with 1 teaspoon of salt. Gradually add about 6 ounces of warm water and knead into a dough—about one minute. Add more flour if the dough is sticky, or more water if it is too dry. Let the dough rest for 15 to 20 minutes. Divide it into eight portions, and roll each portion out on a floured work surface to make a 10-inch circle, ⅛ inch thick. Fry each tortilla in a lightly oiled crepe pan or skillet until bubbles form and the surface is lightly speckled—about 30 seconds. Using a wooden spoon or spatula, flatten the bubbles, then turn the tortilla over and cook for 30 seconds on the other side.*

# Sirloin and Leek Kabobs

Serves 4
Working (and total) time: about 1 hour

Calories **335**
Protein **28g.**
Cholesterol **76mg.**
Total fat **7g.**
Saturated fat **3g.**
Sodium **210mg.**

| |
|---|
| 1¼ lb. boneless sirloin steak, trimmed of fat and cut into long, thin, ½-inch-wide strips |
| ground white pepper |
| 1 tsp. cayenne pepper |
| ½ tsp. ground allspice |
| ½ tsp. ground cumin |
| ½ tsp. turmeric |
| ¼ tsp. salt |
| 3 leeks, washed thoroughly to remove all grit, white parts cut into ½-inch-wide strips, green parts reserved for another use |
| **Ginger chutney** |
| ½ cup golden raisins |
| 2-inch piece fresh ginger, peeled and chopped |
| ½ small onion, chopped |
| 1 tart apple, cored and quartered |
| ½ cup fresh lime juice |
| 1 tbsp. honey |
| ¼ tsp. whole mustard seed |

To make the chutney, chop the raisins, ginger, onion, apple, lime juice, honey, and mustard seed in a food processor or a blender. Transfer the chutney to a bowl and refrigerate it.

If you plan to grill the kabobs, prepare the coals about 30 minutes before cooking time; to broil, preheat the broiler for about 10 minutes.

Combine the white pepper, cayenne pepper, allspice, cumin, turmeric, and salt in a small bowl. Spread the strips of beef on a baking sheet or tray. Using your hands, rub the spice mixture into the beef. Set the beef aside.

Blanch the leeks in a large saucepan of boiling water for two minutes. Drain them and refresh them under cold running water, then drain them again.

Lay a strip of leek on top of each piece of meat. Divide the meat and leeks among 12 skewers, thread-

ing the skewer through both leek and meat at frequent intervals. (If you are using wooden skewers, soak them in water for 10 minutes beforehand.)

Grill or broil the kabobs for one minute on each side for medium-rare meat, and serve them with the ginger chutney.

SUGGESTED ACCOMPANIMENT: *steamed rice tossed with peas.*

## Grilled Sirloin Stuffed with Summer Vegetables

Serves 8
Working time: about 1 hour
Total time: about 2 hours (includes marinating)

Calories **210**
Protein **27g.**
Cholesterol **76mg.**
Total fat **9g.**
Saturated fat **3g.**
Sodium **190mg.**

| |
| --- |
| one 2½-lb. sirloin steak, about 2 inches thick, trimmed of fat |
| 1 tsp. Dijon mustard |
| freshly ground black pepper |
| 1 garlic clove, crushed |
| ⅛ tsp. salt |
| ¼ cup red wine |
| thyme sprigs for garnish (optional) |

| Vegetable stuffing |
| --- |
| 1 tbsp. virgin olive oil |
| ⅓ cup chopped onion |
| 1 sweet green pepper, seeded, deribbed, and diced |
| 1 sweet red pepper, seeded, deribbed, and diced |
| ¼ cup diced zucchini |
| ¼ cup diced yellow squash |
| 2 garlic cloves, finely chopped |
| 1½ tsp. chopped fresh thyme, or ½ tsp. dried thyme leaves |
| 1½ tsp. chopped fresh oregano, or ½ tsp. dried oregano |
| ¼ tsp. hot red-pepper flakes |
| ¼ tsp. salt |
| freshly ground black pepper |
| ¾ cup fresh breadcrumbs |

Using the technique shown below, cut a pocket in the beef. Combine the mustard, pepper, garlic, salt, and wine in a shallow, nonreactive dish. Add the steak to the dish and turn the meat in the marinade once to coat it evenly. Marinate the steak, covered, for one hour at room temperature, turning it several times.

Meanwhile, make the stuffing. Heat the oil in a large, heavy-bottomed skillet over low heat. Add the onion, green and red peppers, zucchini, yellow squash, and garlic. Partially cover the skillet and cook the vegetables, stirring frequently, until they begin to soften—about seven minutes. Add the thyme, oregano, red-pepper flakes, salt, and some black pepper. Stir the mixture well and remove it from the heat. Add the breadcrumbs and toss them with the vegetables. Allow the mixture to cool.

About 30 minutes before cooking the meat, prepare the coals for grilling. When the coals are nearly ready,

remove the meat from the dish, reserving the marinade. Stuff the beef with the cooled vegetable mixture and tie it as demonstrated below.

When the coals are hot, bank them against the sides of the grill. Place a foil drip pan in the center of the coal grate and set the rack in place. Lay the meat in the center of the rack. Grill the meat, basting it occasionally with the reserved marinade, for 20 minutes on the first side. Turn the meat over and continue cooking it for 10 to 20 minutes longer for medium-rare meat.

Remove the meat from the grill and let it stand for 30 minutes. Discard the strings and slice the meat across the grain. Arrange the slices on a platter and serve immediately, garnished with thyme, if you wish. This dish can also be served cold.

SUGGESTED ACCOMPANIMENTS: *grilled sliced potatoes; spinach salad.*

## Cutting and Stuffing a Pocket in a Sirloin Steak

**1** *CUTTING A POCKET. Insert the tip of a knife (here, a boning knife) in the side of a 2-inch-thick boneless sirloin steak. Cut in as deeply as possible without piercing the outer edge of the meat to form a pocket.*

**2** *STUFFING THE POCKET. Using your hands, stuff the prepared filling (recipe, pages 24-25) into the pocket. Be sure to push the filling in as deeply as possible.*

**3** *MAKING THE FIRST LOOP. To keep the pocket from opening during cooking, tie the steak as you would a roast. First, loop butcher's twine around one end of the steak and knot the string, leaving several inches of twine loose at the end.*

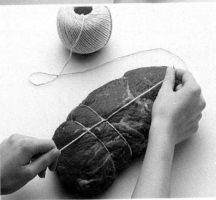

**4** *MAKING SUCCESSIVE LOOPS. With the string still attached to the ball of twine, form a loose loop and twist the string around itself twice. Bring the loop over and under the other end of the meat.*

**5** *TIGHTENING THE STRING. Slide the loop forward so that it rests about 1½ to 2 inches in front of the first loop, and tighten it by pulling both ends of the twine at once. Repeat the process, making three or more loops around the meat and tightening the string after each loop.*

**6** *TYING THE ROAST TOGETHER. Finally, draw the string under the entire length of the meat and back to the first loop you made. Knot the string to the loose length at that end, then sever the string from the ball of twine.*

# Tournedos with Pepper Sauces

Serves 4
Working time: about 1 hour
Total time: about 2 hours and 15 minutes
(includes marinating)

Calories **280**
Protein **26g.**
Cholesterol **73mg.**
Total fat **12g.**
Saturated fat **4g.**
Sodium **190mg.**

| |
| --- |
| one 1¼-lb. beef tenderloin roast, trimmed of fat and cut into 8 small steaks |
| 1 garlic clove, finely chopped |
| 1 cup red wine |
| ½ cup fresh rosemary sprigs, or 1½ tbsp. dried rosemary |
| 3 sweet yellow or green peppers |
| 3 sweet red peppers |
| 2 tsp. red wine vinegar |
| ¼ tsp. salt |
| one 1-lb. eggplant, sliced into 8 rounds |
| 1 tbsp. virgin olive oil |
| 8 rosemary sprigs for garnish (optional) |

Put the steaks into a shallow, nonreactive dish large enough to hold them in a single layer. Sprinkle the chopped garlic, wine, and rosemary over the steaks, and set them aside to marinate at room temperature for two hours.

About one hour before the steaks finish marinating, cook the peppers under a preheated broiler, turning them frequently until their skins blister—about eight minutes. Transfer the peppers to a large bowl and cover the bowl with plastic wrap—the trapped steam will loosen the skins. When the peppers are cool enough to handle, peel, seed, and derib them over a sieve set in a bowl to catch the juices. Cut one of the yellow or green peppers and one of the red peppers into ¼-inch dice; reserve the dice for garnish.

Purée the remaining two yellow or green peppers in a blender or a food processor. Add to the purée 1 teaspoon of the vinegar, ⅛ teaspoon of the salt, and half of the accumulated pepper juices. Pour the purée into a small, nonreactive saucepan and set it aside.

Purée the remaining two red peppers in the blender or food processor; add the remaining teaspoon of vinegar, the other ⅛ teaspoon of salt, and the rest of the pepper juices, and pour this purée into a second small saucepan. Warm both sauces over medium-low heat while you prepare the eggplant and steaks.

With a paring knife, score both sides of each eggplant slice in a crosshatch pattern. Lightly brush both sides with the oil, then broil the slices until they are soft and browned—two to three minutes per side. Remove the slices from the broiler and keep them warm.

Take the steaks out of the marinade and pat them dry; discard the marinade. Broil the steaks until they are medium rare—about three minutes per side.

Place two eggplant slices on each of four dinner plates. Set a steak on each slice of eggplant and spoon the warmed pepper sauces around the steaks. Garnish each portion with the reserved diced sweet peppers—and, if you are using it, a sprig of fresh rosemary—just before serving.

SUGGESTED ACCOMPANIMENT: *sourdough bread.*

# Beef Tenderloin Steaks Stuffed with Oysters and Topped with Kale

THIS NEW DISH CALLS TO MIND AN OLD ONE POPULAR AT THE TURN OF THE CENTURY, BEEFSTEAK WITH OYSTER BLANKET, IN WHICH THE OYSTERS WERE SERVED ON TOP OF THE MEAT.

Serves 6
Working (and total time): about 1 hour

Calories **165**
Protein **23g.**
Cholesterol **77mg.**
Total fat **6g.**
Saturated fat **2g.**
Sodium **195mg.**

| |
| --- |
| 6 tenderloin steaks (about 4 oz. each), trimmed of fat |
| 12 shucked oysters, with their liquid |
| 6 shallots, finely chopped |
| 3 tbsp. champagne vinegar or red wine vinegar |
| ¼ cup unsalted brown stock or unsalted chicken stock (recipes, page 138) |
| 3 cups coarsely shredded, tightly packed kale |
| ¼ tsp. salt |
| freshly ground black pepper |

If you plan to grill the steaks, prepare the coals about 30 minutes before cooking time; to broil, preheat the broiler for about 10 minutes.

Poach the oysters in their liquid in a small saucepan over medium heat just until their edges curl—about ▶

one minute. With a slotted spoon, remove the oysters from the pan and set them aside. Strain the poaching liquid and reserve it.

Cut a slit in the side of each steak to make a pocket large enough to hold one of the oysters. Stuff the steaks with six of the oysters.

Cook the steaks on the grill or under the broiler for two to three minutes on each side for medium-rare steaks. Set the steaks aside in a warm place.

Heat the shallots, vinegar, and stock in a large, heavy-bottomed, nonreactive skillet over medium-high heat until the liquid boils. Cook the mixture until it has reduced by one-third—three to four minutes. Stir in the kale, the remaining oysters, the poaching liquid, the salt, and some pepper. Toss the mixture until the greens begin to wilt—about two minutes.

Spoon the kale and oysters over the steaks and serve immediately.

SUGGESTED ACCOMPANIMENT: *baked potatoes.*

# Skewered Beef with Julienned Papaya

Serves 8 as a main course or 16 as an appetizer
Working time: about 35 minutes
Total time: about 1 hour and 35 minutes
(includes marinating)

Calories **265**
Protein **25g.**
Cholesterol **54mg.**
Total fat **10g.**
Saturated fat **3g.**
Sodium **280mg.**

| |
|---|
| 2 lb. top round steak, trimmed of fat |
| 2 underripe papayas, or 4 mangoes, halved, seeded, and julienned |
| 2 tbsp. fresh lime juice |
| 32 cherry tomatoes, halved lengthwise |
| 2 scallions, green parts only, thinly sliced |
| 2 tbsp. crushed unsalted roasted peanuts |
| **Spicy peanut marinade** |
| 2½ tbsp. low-sodium soy sauce |
| 2 scallions, white parts only, thinly sliced |
| 1½ tbsp. finely chopped fresh ginger |
| 3 garlic cloves, finely chopped |
| 2 small dried red chili peppers, chopped (cautionary note, page 8), or ¼ tsp. hot red-pepper flakes |
| 3 tbsp. unsalted peanut butter |
| ¼ cup plain low-fat yogurt |
| 2 tbsp. dry white wine |
| 2 tbsp. fresh lime juice |
| 1 tbsp. honey |

To make the marinade, combine the soy sauce with the scallions, ginger, garlic, and chili peppers or pepper flakes in a large bowl. Let the mixture stand for one minute, then whisk in the peanut butter, yogurt, wine, lime juice, and honey.

Slice the beef into strips about 5 inches long and ⅛ inch thick—you will need 32 slices. Toss the beef strips in the marinade and allow them to sit for one hour at room temperature.

While the beef is marinating, combine the papaya or mango julienne and the lime juice in a bowl. Refrigerate the fruit mixture.

If you plan to grill the beef, prepare the coals in an outdoor grill about 30 minutes before cooking time; to broil, preheat the broiler for 10 minutes. Soak 32 wooden skewers in water for 10 minutes.

Thread a skewer through a tomato half, then through a strip of beef; finish with another tomato half. Repeat the process for the remaining tomatoes and beef strips. Brush the skewered meat and tomatoes with any remaining marinade.

Cook the meat, on one side only, in two batches until it begins to brown—four to six minutes. Transfer the skewers to a serving platter.

Sprinkle the meat with the scallion greens and peanuts, and serve the chilled papaya or mango alongside.

SUGGESTED ACCOMPANIMENT: *roasted peppers.*

## Veal Steaks Teriyaki

THIS RECIPE IS BASED ON THE JAPANESE "TERIYAKI" STYLE OF MARINATING MEAT IN A MIXTURE OF MIRIN, SOY SAUCE, AND FRESH GINGER. THE LONG MARINATING TENDERIZES THE MEAT, WITH SUCCULENT RESULTS.

Serves 4
Working time: about 20 minutes
Total time: about 25 hours (includes marinating)

| | |
|---|---|
| Calories **185** | one 1-lb. piece loin of veal, cut diagonally into 8 pieces |
| Protein **26g.** | |
| Cholesterol **90mg.** | ¼ cup low-sodium soy sauce |
| Total fat **7g.** | 2 tbsp. mirin (Japanese sweet rice wine) or sweet sherry |
| Saturated fat **2g.** | |
| Sodium **150mg.** | 1-inch piece fresh ginger, peeled and finely chopped |
| | 4 garlic cloves, crushed |
| | 1 tsp. light brown sugar |
| | 1 tbsp. peanut oil |
| | ⅔ cup unsalted chicken stock (recipe, page 138) |
| | scallions or celery cut into brooms for garnish |

In a small bowl, whisk the soy sauce with the mirin or sherry, ginger, garlic, and sugar. Put the pieces of veal into a shallow, nonreactive dish and pour the marinade over them. Turn the veal several times to ensure that the pieces are evenly coated. Cover the veal and let it marinate in the refrigerator for 24 to 36 hours, turning it occasionally. Thirty minutes before cooking, remove the veal from the refrigerator and let it come to room temperature. Ten minutes before cooking, preheat the broiler.

Remove the veal from the marinade, brushing off and reserving any excess marinade. Brush the veal on both sides with the oil, then place the veal on the broiler rack. Broil for two to three minutes, then turn and broil for another two to three minutes.

Meanwhile, transfer the marinade to a small, non-reactive saucepan and add the stock. Bring the liquid to a boil, skim it, then simmer it over low heat for two minutes. Serve the steaks hot with the sauce poured over them, garnished with scallion or celery brooms.

SUGGESTED ACCOMPANIMENTS: *rice; stir-fried snow peas and sweet red peppers.*

# Veal Chops Dijonnaise

Serves 4
Working time: about 15 minutes
Total time: about 2 hours and 15 minutes
(includes marinating)

Calories **255**
Protein **23g.**
Cholesterol **120mg.**
Total fat **16g.**
Saturated fat **5g.**
Sodium **120mg.**

| |
|---|
| 4 veal chops (6 to 7 oz. each), trimmed of fat |
| 3 tbsp. capers, drained and crushed |
| 2 tbsp. virgin olive oil |
| 2 tbsp. fresh lemon juice |
| 2 tsp. Dijon mustard |
| 2 tsp. chopped fresh tarragon, or 1 tsp. dried tarragon |
| freshly ground black pepper |
| tarragon sprigs for garnish (optional) |

Place the chops side by side in a shallow, nonreactive dish. In a mixing bowl, whisk together the capers, oil, lemon juice, mustard, tarragon, and some black pepper. Brush the mixture over both sides of the chops. Cover the chops and let them marinate in the refrigerator for two hours.

Preheat the broiler. Place the chops on the broiler rack and broil for four minutes, basting frequently with the marinade. Turn the chops over and broil for another four minutes, again basting them with the marinade. Pour the cooking juices from the broiler pan over the chops and garnish them with the tarragon sprigs, if desired. Serve hot.

SUGGESTED ACCOMPANIMENTS: *green salad; mushrooms cooked in lemon juice.*

## Paupiettes of Veal in Avgolemono Sauce

THE SAUCE IS BASED ON THE EGG AND LEMON SOUP OF
THE SAME NAME: ITS SHARP, LEMONY FLAVOR ADDS PIQUANCY
TO THE VEAL AND STUFFING.

Serves 4
Working (and total) time: about 1 hour

| | |
|---|---|
| Calories **285** | 4 veal cutlets (3 to 4 oz. each), trimmed |
| Protein **28g.** | of fat and flattened |
| Cholesterol **135mg.** | (page 32, Step 1) |
| Total fat **11g.** | 3 small red onions, cut into eighths |
| Saturated fat **3g.** | 1 tbsp. virgin olive oil |
| Sodium **355mg.** | freshly ground black pepper |

**Anchovy stuffing**

6 canned anchovy fillets, soaked in 6 tbsp. of milk
for 20 minutes, drained, rinsed,
and patted dry

1 cup fresh whole-wheat breadcrumbs

1 lemon, grated zest only

2 tbsp. lemon juice

4 tsp. chopped fresh chervil or parsley
(or a mixture of the two)

freshly ground black pepper

**Avgolemono sauce**

1¼ cups unsalted chicken stock (recipe, page 138)

1 egg yolk

1 lemon, juice only

1 tsp. arrowroot

freshly ground black pepper

Slice each cutlet into 4 equal pieces (page 32, Step 2), making 16 pieces in all. Soak eight bamboo skewers in water for 10 minutes.

To make the stuffing, coarsely chop the anchovy fillets and put them into a bowl. Add the breadcrumbs, lemon zest and juice, chervil or parsley, and some pepper. Preheat the broiler. Spoon one-sixteenth of the stuffing onto each piece of veal.

Roll the veal up around the stuffing, tucking in any ends of meat if necessary (page 32, Step 3), then squeeze the paupiettes gently in your hands so that they hold together. Thread two paupiettes onto each of eight bamboo skewers, alternating with onion sections. Place the skewers on the broiler rack, brush with half of the oil, and sprinkle with some pepper. Broil for two to three minutes. Turn, brush with the remaining oil, sprinkle with pepper, and broil for two to three minutes more.

To make the sauce, put the stock into a small, non-reactive saucepan and bring it to a boil. Remove it from the heat. In a bowl, mix together the egg yolk, lemon juice, and arrowroot. Stir in a few spoonfuls of the hot stock, then pour this mixture into the remaining stock in the pan. Bring to just below the boiling point and simmer, whisking vigorously, until the sauce thickens—two to three minutes. Add some black pepper.

Pour some sauce onto four individual plates, and arrange the paupiettes and onions on top.

SUGGESTED ACCOMPANIMENTS: watercress and green grape salad; tomato salad.

## Flattening, Stuffing, and Rolling Veal Slices

**1** *FLATTENING THE MEAT. Trim each cutlet of excess fat and lay it between two sheets of plastic wrap. With a meat bat or rolling pin, flatten the cutlet by gently tapping until the meat is of an even thickness. Vigorous pounding will make the veal dry.*

**2** *SLICING THE CUTLETS. Slice each flattened cutlet into four pieces. Put about a tablespoon of stuffing on one end of a piece.*

**3** *ROLLING AND SECURING THE SLICES. Roll up the meat, starting at the end nearest the stuffing. Squeeze the roll gently to help the stuffing adhere to the meat. Secure the rolls with a bamboo skewer, or alternatively, pin each one with a toothpick.*

# Grilled Veal with Spicy Orange Sauce

Serves 8
Working time: about 1 hour
Total time: about 3 hours (includes marinating)

Calories **230**
Protein **22g.**
Cholesterol **90mg.**
Total fat **10g.**
Saturated fat **3g.**
Sodium **160mg.**

| |
|---|
| one 2-lb. piece veal rump, trimmed |
| 1 tsp. whole allspice |
| 1 tsp. juniper berries |
| 2 tbsp. virgin olive oil |
| ¼ tsp. salt |
| freshly ground black pepper |
| 2 oranges, finely grated zest only |
| **Spicy orange sauce** |
| 1 cup fresh orange juice |
| ¼ cup honey |
| 2 tbsp. red wine vinegar |
| 2 garlic cloves, crushed |
| one 14-oz. can tomatoes, drained and sieved |
| 1 tbsp. orange-flavored liqueur |
| ½ tsp. paprika |
| hot red-pepper sauce |
| ¼ tsp. salt |
| freshly ground black pepper |

To prepare the marinade, place the allspice and juniper berries in a mortar and crush them with a pestle, then blend in the olive oil, salt, some freshly ground black pepper, and the orange zest.

Place the veal in a shallow dish, pour the marinade over it, and coat it well. Cover and marinate at room temperature for two to three hours.

To prepare the sauce, put the orange juice, honey, wine vinegar, garlic, tomatoes, and orange-flavored liqueur into a nonreactive, heavy-bottomed saucepan. Add the paprika, a few drops of hot red-pepper sauce, the salt, and some pepper. Bring to a boil, then lower the heat and simmer very gently for 45 minutes to one hour, until the sauce is reduced and thickened.

Light the charcoal in the grill about 30 minutes before you plan to cook the veal. Skewer the meat into a neat shape using one or two large metal skewers. Cook the veal on a rack over medium-hot coals, turning it frequently until it is cooked through but still slightly pink inside—35 to 45 minutes—taking care that the veal does not burn.

To serve, slide the veal off the skewers onto a cutting board and cut into thin slices. Serve with the sauce.

SUGGESTED ACCOMPANIMENTS: *salad; whole-grain bread.*

EDITOR'S NOTE: *The sauce can be served either hot or cold.*

## Broiled Veal Chops with Shallots and Fennel

Serves 4
Working (and total) time: about 30 minutes

Calories **265**
Protein **25g.**
Cholesterol **110mg.**
Total fat **15g.**
Saturated fat **5g.**
Sodium **260mg.**

| |
|---|
| 4 veal rib chops (about ½ lb. each), cut between the bones, about ½ inch thick |
| 2 tbsp. virgin olive oil |
| 1 tsp. grated lemon zest |
| ½ lemon, juice only |
| 1 large garlic clove, finely chopped |
| 3 shallots, finely chopped |
| 1 tbsp. chopped fresh parsley |
| 1 tsp. chopped fresh rosemary, or ½ tsp. dried rosemary, crumbled |
| freshly ground black pepper |
| 1 fennel bulb, very finely julienned |
| 4 cups kale, washed, trimmed, and finely shredded |
| ¼ tsp. salt |
| lemon wedges for garnish |

Preheat the broiler. Combine the oil, lemon zest and juice, garlic, shallots, parsley, rosemary, and some pepper in a small bowl. Arrange the chops side by side on a rack in a broiler pan. Brush the tops with about a quarter of the lemon-shallot mixture and broil for about three minutes or until golden brown. Turn the chops over and brush with another quarter of the lemon-shallot mixture. Broil for three minutes more.

Mix the fennel into the remaining lemon-shallot mixture and spoon it on top of the chops. Press down lightly to smooth out any pieces of fennel that might be sticking up. Continue broiling for about five minutes, or until the fennel mixture is golden brown.

Meanwhile, cook the shredded kale in a vegetable steamer for two to three minutes, or until it is just tender. Add the salt to the kale and toss.

Spread out the kale in an even layer on a large serving platter. Arrange the chops on top and garnish with lemon wedges. Serve hot.

SUGGESTED ACCOMPANIMENT: *boiled new potatoes.*

# Veal, Chicken, and Eggplant Kabobs with Strawberry and Cucumber Sauce

Serves 4
Working time: about 1 hour
Total time: about 1 hour and 40 minutes

Calories **200**
Protein **25g.**
Cholesterol **75mg.**
Total fat **5g.**
Saturated fat **2g.**
Sodium **295mg.**

| |
|---|
| 6 oz. veal top round or rump, trimmed of fat and ground or chopped (technique, page 15) |
| 6 oz. chicken breast meat, ground |
| 1 small eggplant (about 6 oz.), peeled and chopped |
| 1¼ tsp. salt |
| 1 large sweet red pepper |
| 1 garlic clove, chopped |
| freshly ground black pepper |
| ½ lemon, grated zest only |
| 2 tbsp. chopped fresh mint |
| 1 tbsp. chopped fresh parsley |
| ⅓ to ⅔ cup fresh breadcrumbs |
| 8 large black olives, pitted |
| **Strawberry and cucumber sauce** |
| ½ medium cucumber |
| ⅔ cup plain low-fat yogurt |
| ½ cup strawberries, hulled and finely chopped |
| 2 tbsp. finely sliced fresh mint |

Put the eggplant into a colander, sprinkle it with 1 teaspoon of the salt, and weight it down with a plate. Let it drain for 20 minutes.

Meanwhile, make the sauce. Grate the cucumber, then wrap it in paper towels and squeeze out the excess moisture. Put the cucumber into a bowl, add the yogurt, strawberries, and mint, and stir together. Cover and chill.

Place the pepper about 2 inches below a preheated broiler, turning it from time to time until the skin becomes blistered. Put the pepper into a bowl, cover with plastic wrap, and let it cool; the steam trapped inside will loosen the skin. Peel the pepper, remove the stem, ribs, and seeds, and cut it into 1-inch squares.

To make the kabobs, rinse the eggplant and squeeze it dry in your hands. Put the eggplant into a food processor, add the garlic, and blend until smooth. Transfer the eggplant purée to a bowl, and add the veal, the chicken, the remaining salt, some black pepper, the lemon zest, the mint, and the parsley. Mix well together with your hands, then work in enough breadcrumbs to make the mixture firm. Shape into walnut-size balls and chill for 30 minutes.

Preheat the broiler. Thread the meatballs, squares of red pepper, and the olives onto four metal skewers. Broil for 15 to 20 minutes, turning the skewers to cook and brown them evenly.

Serve the kabobs immediately, accompanied by the strawberry and cucumber sauce.

SUGGESTED ACCOMPANIMENTS: *green salad; pita bread.*
EDITOR'S NOTE: *These kabobs can also be cooked on a grill.*

# Veal and Apricot Brochettes Tikka-Style

Serves 4
Working time: about 30 minutes
Total time: about 6 hours and 45 minutes
(includes marinating)

Calories **180**
Protein **20g.**
Cholesterol **75mg.**
Total fat **5g.**
Saturated fat **2g.**
Sodium **240mg.**

| |
|---|
| ¾ lb. veal top round, rump, or boned loin, trimmed of fat and cut into 1-inch cubes |
| 16 dried apricot halves |
| 2 small zucchini, trimmed and cut into chunks |
| lime wedges or slices for garnish |
| **Spicy yogurt marinade** |
| 1¼ cups plain low-fat yogurt |
| 1 small onion, chopped |
| 1 garlic clove, chopped |
| ½-inch piece fresh ginger, peeled, or 1 tbsp. freshly grated ginger |
| 1 lime, juice only |
| 2 cardamom pods |
| 1 small dried red chili pepper (cautionary note, page 8) |
| 4 whole cloves |
| 6 black peppercorns |
| ¼-inch piece cinnamon stick |
| 1 tsp. freshly grated or ground nutmeg |
| ¼ tsp. coriander seeds |
| ¼ tsp. cumin seeds |

¼ tsp. salt

First make the marinade. Combine the yogurt, chopped onion, garlic, ginger, and lime juice in a food processor and blend the mixture until it is quite smooth. Strain it into a bowl.

Break open the cardamom pods and put the seeds into a mortar. Add the chili pepper, cloves, peppercorns, cinnamon stick, nutmeg, coriander seeds, and cumin seeds. Pound these ingredients with a pestle until they are fine. Alternatively, the spices may be worked in a spice grinder. Add the spices and the salt to the yogurt mixture and stir well. Add the cubes of veal and the apricots, and coat them in the mixture. Cover the veal and let it marinate in the refrigerator for at least six hours, stirring occasionally.

Preheat the broiler. Thread the veal cubes, apricots, and zucchini onto four or eight skewers, shaking off and reserving any excess marinade. (If you are using wooden skewers, soak them in water for 10 minutes beforehand.) Grill the kabobs for about 15 minutes, turning them to cook and brown evenly.

While the kabobs are cooking, strain the marinade through a fine sieve into a small, heavy-bottomed, nonreactive saucepan. Heat the marinade through very gently, stirring occasionally; do not let it boil. Serve the kabobs garnished with lime wedges or slices, and pass the heated marinade sauce separately.

SUGGESTED ACCOMPANIMENTS: *saffron rice; a salad of tomatoes and onions.*

## Roulades Stuffed with Watercress and Walnuts

Serves 8
Working (and total) time: about 40 minutes

Calories **190**
Protein **22g.**
Cholesterol **61mg.**
Total fat **11g.**
Saturated fat **2g.**
Sodium **145mg.**

| |
|---|
| one 2-lb. bottom round steak, about 1 inch thick, trimmed of fat |
| 2 bunches watercress, washed and stemmed |
| 1 lb. spinach, washed and stemmed |
| 1 tbsp. virgin olive oil |
| ¼ cup finely chopped walnuts |
| 1 tbsp. finely chopped fresh rosemary, or 1½ tsp. dried rosemary |
| 2 anchovies, rinsed, patted dry, and finely chopped |
| ¼ tsp. salt |
| freshly ground black pepper |

Cut the steak in half across its width. Then, holding your knife blade parallel to the work surface, slice through both halves horizontally to form eight ¼-inch-thick slices. (Alternatively, ask the butcher to slice the meat for you.)

Place a slice of beef between two sheets of plastic wrap and flatten it to ⅛-inch thickness by pounding first one side and then the other with a meat mallet or the flat of a heavy knife. Flatten the remaining seven pieces in the same manner. Set the beef aside while you prepare the stuffing.

Bring 2 quarts of water to a boil in a large pot. Plunge the watercress into the boiling water and cook it for 30 seconds. Add the spinach, stir well, and cook the greens for 15 seconds longer. Drain the spinach and watercress, and squeeze them firmly into a ball to extract as much moisture as possible. Finely chop the ball of greens.

Heat ½ tablespoon of the oil in a heavy-bottomed skillet over medium heat. Add the walnuts, rosemary, and anchovies. Cook the mixture, stirring, for one minute. Stir in the greens, the salt, and some pepper. Remove the skillet from the heat.

Preheat the oven to 425° F. Spread 2 tablespoons of the stuffing on each piece of meat, leaving a ¼-inch border around the edges. Roll up the pieces, starting at a long edge, and set the roulades seam down on a broiler pan at least 1 inch apart.

Brush the roulades with the remaining ½ tablespoon of the oil. Bake them for 15 minutes. Remove the pan from the oven and allow the meat to stand for five minutes. Cut each roulade on the diagonal into six to eight thin slices.

SUGGESTED ACCOMPANIMENT: *steamed baby turnips.*

# Roast Sirloin of Beef with Yorkshire Pudding

COOKING A BEEF ROAST IN A ROASTING BAG ENSURES A MOIST, SUCCULENT RESULT. YORKSHIRE PUDDING MADE WITH OLIVE OIL INSTEAD OF DRIPPINGS AND WITH A MIXTURE OF MILK AND WATER IS LIGHT AND FLUFFY—AND LOW IN SATURATED FAT.

Serves 6
Working time: about 30 minutes
Total time: about 1 hour and 15 minutes

Calories **345**
Protein **40g.**
Cholesterol **115mg.**
Total fat **15g.**
Saturated fat **5g.**
Sodium **133mg.**

| |
|---|
| one 2 to 2¼-lb. beef sirloin roast, boned, trimmed of fat, rolled and tied |
| 1 tbsp. grated fresh horseradish |
| 2 tsp. grainy mustard |
| 4 tsp. unbleached all-purpose flour |
| 1¼ cups brown stock (recipe, page 138) |
| **Yorkshire pudding** |
| ½ cup unbleached all-purpose flour |
| ⅛ tsp. salt |
| freshly ground black pepper |
| 1 egg, beaten |
| ½ cup low-fat milk |
| 1½ tbsp. virgin olive oil |

Preheat the oven to 375° F.

Mix together the horseradish and mustard, and brush the mixture over the top of the roast. Dust the inside of a roasting bag with 1 teaspoon of the flour (to help prevent spattering during cooking), then place the roast in the bag with the horseradish and mustard mixture on top of the roast. Seal the bag according to the manufacturer's instructions, leaving an opening for steam to escape.

Place the bag in a roasting pan, making sure the opening in the bag faces up so that the cooking juices do not run out. Allow 15 minutes roasting time per 1 pound for rare meat, 20 minutes for medium, and 25 minutes for well done.

Meanwhile, make the batter for the Yorkshire pudding. Sift the flour, salt, and some pepper into a bowl, make a well in the center, and add the egg. Put the milk into a measuring cup, add enough cold water to make ⅔ cup, and then gradually whisk the liquid into the flour and egg. Beat well to remove any lumps. Cover the bowl and set it aside until you are ready to cook the pudding.

Remove the roast from the oven but leave it in the bag. Increase the oven temperature to 425° F. Brush the oil over the inside of a muffin pan (or 12 individual muffin cups) and place the pan in the hottest part of the oven until it is smoking hot—three to five minutes. Remove the muffin pan from the oven, whisk the batter, and pour it into the pan. Return it to the hottest part of the oven and cook for 15 to 20 minutes, or until the pudding is golden and well risen. Do not open the oven door during this time or the pudding will collapse.

While the Yorkshire pudding is cooking, remove the roast from the bag, put it onto a heated platter, and keep it warm. Pour the cooking juices into a saucepan, add the stock, and bring to a boil. Mix the remaining 3 teaspoons of flour with 1 tablespoon of cold water, add a few spoonfuls of the hot stock, then stir into the pan. Simmer, stirring, until the gravy reduces and thickens—about five minutes. Pour into a gravy boat.

When the Yorkshire pudding is ready, arrange it around the roast beef or place it on a warmed serving dish. Carve the meat at the table and pass the gravy separately.

SUGGESTED ACCOMPANIMENT: *green beans.*

# Beef Tenderloin and Potato Roast

Serves 4
Working time: about 20 minutes
Total time: about 1 hour and 15 minutes

Calories **290**
Protein **27g.**
Cholesterol **73mg.**
Total fat **9g.**
Saturated fat **3g.**
Sodium **145mg.**

| |
|---|
| one 1¼-lb. beef tenderloin roast, trimmed of fat and cut into 8 slices |
| ½ tsp. ground allspice |
| ¼ cup chopped fresh parsley, plus sprig for garnish |
| 1 tbsp. red wine vinegar |
| ⅛ tsp. salt |
| 1 lb. baking potatoes, scrubbed and cut into ¼-inch-thick slices |
| 2 onions, thinly sliced |
| ½ cup unsalted brown stock or unsalted chicken stock (recipes, page 138) |

Preheat the oven to 350° F.

Mix the allspice, 2 tablespoons of the parsley, the vinegar, and the salt in a small bowl. Using your hands, rub this mixture into the beef slices and place them in a shallow, nonreactive dish. Let the meat marinate at room temperature while you prepare the potatoes.

Combine the potatoes and onions in a flameproof baking dish. Pour in the stock and 1 cup of water. Bring the liquid to a boil over medium-high heat, then bake the potatoes in the oven until they are tender and have browned—about 45 minutes. (If you do not have a flameproof baking dish, bring the potatoes, onions, stock, and water to a boil in a saucepan, then transfer the mixture to a baking dish, and proceed as above.)

When the potatoes are cooked, remove the dish from the oven and increase the temperature to 450° F.

Heat a nonstick skillet over medium-high heat. Pat the beef slices dry with paper towels and sear them for 30 seconds on each side. Set the beef on top of the potatoes and return the dish to the oven. Bake the beef and potatoes for three minutes; turn the meat and bake it for three minutes more.

Sprinkle the remaining 2 tablespoons of chopped parsley over the top before serving the dish, garnished with the sprig of parsley.

SUGGESTED ACCOMPANIMENT: *steamed Brussels sprouts.*

## Layered Meat Loaf

Serves 8
Working time: about 40 minutes
Total time: about 2 hours

Calories **220**
Protein **23g.**
Cholesterol **56mg.**
Total fat **8g.**
Saturated fat **3g.**
Sodium **230mg.**

| |
|---|
| 1¾ lb. beef round, trimmed of fat and ground or chopped (technique, page 15) |
| 2 large ripe tomatoes (about 1 lb.), peeled, seeded, and chopped |
| 1 onion, chopped |
| 3 garlic cloves, finely chopped |
| 1½ tsp. chopped fresh oregano, or ½ tsp. dried oregano |
| ½ cup port or Madeira |
| 2 tbsp. red wine vinegar |
| 1 tbsp. sugar |
| ¼ tsp. salt |
| freshly ground black pepper |
| 6 tbsp. freshly grated Parmesan cheese |
| ⅔ cup dry breadcrumbs |
| 1 egg white |
| 1 tbsp. safflower oil |
| 2 bunches watercress, trimmed and washed |
| 1 tbsp. chopped fresh thyme, or 1 tsp. dried thyme leaves |

Heat a large, heavy-bottomed, nonreactive skillet over medium-high heat. Add the tomatoes, onion, garlic, and oregano. Cook the vegetables, stirring occasionally, for five minutes. Add the port or Madeira, vinegar, sugar, ⅛ teaspoon of the salt, and some pepper. Cook the mixture until almost all of the liquid has evapo-rated—about 10 minutes. Purée the mixture and place all but ¼ cup of it in a large bowl.

Preheat the oven to 400° F. Add the beef, 4 table-spoons of the grated cheese, ⅓ cup of the bread-crumbs, the remaining ⅛ teaspoon of salt, some pep-per, and the egg white to the tomato mixture in the bowl. Mix the ingredients well and set the meat aside while you prepare the watercress.

Heat the oil in a large, heavy-bottomed skillet over high heat. Add the watercress, thyme, and some pep-per. Cook, stirring constantly, until the watercress has wilted and almost all of the liquid has evaporated—three to four minutes. Chop the watercress finely. Place it in a bowl and combine it with the remaining ⅓ cup of breadcrumbs.

To layer the meat loaf, divide the beef mixture into three equal portions. Using a rolling pin or your hands, flatten each portion into a rectangle 5 inches wide, 8 inches long, and ¾ inch thick.

Place one rectangle in a shallow baking pan. Top it with half of the watercress mixture, spreading the watercress evenly over the surface. Lay another rec-tangle on top and cover it with the remaining water-cress. Finish with the final rectangle, then spread the reserved tomato sauce over the top and sides of the loaf. Sprinkle on the remaining Parmesan cheese, and bake the meat loaf for one hour and 10 minutes. Let the meat loaf stand for 10 minutes, then carefully transfer it to a platter, slice it, and serve.

SUGGESTED ACCOMPANIMENT: *boiled new potatoes.*

# Rump Roast with Winter Vegetables

Serves 8
Working time: about 20 minutes
Total time: about 2 hours

Calories **205**
Protein **24g.**
Cholesterol **60mg.**
Total fat **7g.**
Saturated fat **2g.**
Sodium **165mg.**

| |
|---|
| one 2¼-lb. rump roast, trimmed of fat |
| 1 tsp. safflower oil |
| ¼ tsp. salt |
| ½ tsp. cracked black peppercorns |
| 1 garlic clove, finely chopped |
| 2 large carrots, peeled and sliced into ¾-inch-thick rounds |
| 2 large turnips, peeled and cut into ½-inch-thick wedges |
| 1 rutabaga, peeled and cut into ¾-inch cubes |
| ½ lb. white onions, cut into eighths |
| ½ tbsp. chopped fresh thyme, or ¾ tsp. dried thyme leaves |
| 4 tsp. cornstarch |
| ¼ cup low-fat milk |
| 2 tsp. grainy mustard |

Preheat the oven to 325° F.

Heat a large, nonstick skillet over medium-high heat. Add the oil, tilting the pan to coat the bottom. Sear the roast in the pan—approximately one minute on each side.

Transfer the meat to a roasting pan, sprinkle the meat with the salt, peppercorns, and garlic, and roast the beef until it is medium rare and registers 140° F. on a meat thermometer—about one hour and 15 minutes. Remove the roast from the pan and set it aside. Skim and discard any fat from the juices in the pan; set the pan with its juices aside.

Toss the carrots, turnips, rutabaga, and onions with the thyme. Pour enough water into a large pot to fill it 1 inch deep. Place a vegetable steamer in the pot and bring the water to a boil. Put the vegetables into the steamer, cover the pot, and cook the vegetables until they are tender—about 10 minutes. Remove the vegetables from the steamer and keep them warm.

Pour about 1 cup of the steaming liquid into the roasting pan. Simmer the liquid over medium-high heat, stirring constantly to dissolve any caramelized roasting juices on the bottom of the pan. Mix the cornstarch and milk in a small bowl, then whisk this mixture into the simmering liquid. Stir the liquid until the sauce thickens, then whisk in the mustard. Remove the pan from the heat and keep it warm.

Slice the roast and arrange the slices on a platter. Toss the vegetables with some of the sauce and place them around the meat. Serve the roast with the remaining sauce passed separately.

SUGGESTED ACCOMPANIMENT: *steamed kale or spinach.*

# Spicy Beef Salad

Serves 4
Working time: about 25 minutes
Total time: about 2 hours and 45 minutes
(includes marinating)

Calories **295**
Protein **22g.**
Cholesterol **57mg.**
Total fat **5g.**
Saturated fat **2g.**
Sodium **120mg.**

| |
| --- |
| one 1-lb. boneless sirloin steak, trimmed of fat |
| 8 whole cloves |
| 8 black peppercorns |
| 12 whole allspice |
| 1 large onion, thinly sliced |
| 2 tbsp. brandy |
| 2 cups red wine |
| 6 oz. mixed dried fruit, coarsely chopped |
| ¼ cup red wine vinegar |
| 1 cinnamon stick |
| 1 lb. turnips, peeled, halved lengthwise, and sliced |
| ¼ cup chopped fresh parsley |
| watercress sprigs, trimmed, washed, and dried, for garnish (optional) |

Put the steak into a shallow pan with the cloves, peppercorns, whole allspice, onion slices, brandy, and 1 cup of the wine. Let the steak marinate at room temperature for two hours, turning it every now and then.

In a nonreactive saucepan, combine the dried fruit with the vinegar, the remaining cup of wine, 1 cup of water, and the cinnamon stick. Bring the liquid to a boil, then lower the heat and simmer the mixture for 30 minutes. Drain the fruit in a sieve set over a bowl; discard the cinnamon stick and set the fruit aside. Return the liquid to the saucepan and boil it until it is reduced by about half—approximately five minutes.

Preheat the oven to 475° F. Pour enough water into a saucepan to fill it about 1 inch deep. Set a vegetable steamer in the pan and bring the water to a boil. Put the turnips into the steamer, cover them, and steam them until they are tender—about 10 minutes. Transfer the turnips to a bowl and set them aside.

Remove the steak from the marinade and pat it dry with paper towels; discard the marinade. Roast the steak for 15 minutes, then remove it from the oven and let it rest for 30 minutes. Cut the steak against the grain into slices about ¼ inch thick. Cut each slice into strips about 1½ inches long.

Toss the strips of beef with the reduced wine mixture, the parsley, the turnips, and the reserved fruit. Arrange the salad on a platter; garnish it with watercress, if you like, and serve.

SUGGESTED ACCOMPANIMENT: *small whole-wheat dinner rolls.*

## Skewered Meatballs with Eggplant Relish

Serves 8
Working time: about 1 hour
Total time: about 1 hour and 30 minutes

Calories **235**
Protein **26g.**
Cholesterol **61mg.**
Total fat **7g.**
Saturated fat **2g.**
Sodium **190mg.**

| | |
|---|---|
| 2¼ lb. beef round, trimmed of fat and ground or chopped (technique, page 15) | |
| 2 eggplants (about 2 lb.), pierced in several places with a knife | |
| 2 onions, finely chopped | |
| 6 garlic cloves, finely chopped | |

| |
|---|
| 1 tsp. virgin olive oil |
| 4 tbsp. chopped fresh mint, or 2 tsp. dried oregano |
| 3 tbsp. fresh lemon juice |
| ¼ tsp. salt |
| freshly ground black pepper |
| 4 slices whole-wheat bread |
| 5 tbsp. chopped fresh parsley |
| mint sprigs for garnish (optional) |
| ½ cup plain low-fat yogurt |

Preheat the oven to 500° F. Roast the eggplants in the oven, turning them occasionally, until they are blistered on all sides—about 20 minutes. Transfer the ▶

eggplants to a bowl, cover it with plastic wrap, and refrigerate it.

Simmer the onion, garlic, oil, and ¼ cup of water in a heavy-bottomed saucepan until the onion is translucent—about five minutes. Increase the heat and boil until the water has evaporated—about one minute.

To prepare the relish, peel the skin from the eggplants, and purée the flesh in a blender or a food processor. Remove ¼ cup of the eggplant purée and set it aside. In a small bowl, combine the rest of the eggplant with the chopped mint or dried oregano, the lemon juice, half of the onion and garlic mixture, ⅛ teaspoon of the salt, and a generous grinding of pepper. Put the eggplant relish into the refrigerator.

Soak the bread for in water for three minutes. Using your hands, gently squeeze the water from the bread.

Mix the ground beef, the bread, the parsley, the rest of the onion and garlic mixture, the reserved ¼ cup of eggplant purée, the remaining ⅛ teaspoon of salt, and a generous grinding of black pepper. Form the meat mixture into 48 balls. Thread three meatballs on each of 16 skewers and set them on a baking sheet. (If you are using wooden skewers, soak them for 10 minutes beforehand.) Cook the meatballs in the oven until they are browned—10 to 15 minutes.

Arrange the meatballs on a platter, garnished, if you like, with mint sprigs. Put the yogurt into a small bowl, and pass the eggplant relish and the yogurt separately.

SUGGESTED ACCOMPANIMENT: *pita bread.*

# Mediterranean Meat Loaf

Serves 10
Working time: about 1 hour
Total time: about 2 hours

Calories **220**
Protein **22g.**
Cholesterol **50mg.**
Total fat **6g.**
Saturated fat **2g.**
Sodium **140mg.**

| |
|---|
| 2¼ lb. beef round, trimmed of fat and ground or chopped (technique, page 15) |
| 1 tsp. virgin olive oil |
| 2 carrots, finely chopped |
| 2 celery stalks, finely chopped |
| 2 onions, finely chopped |
| 1 lb. eggplant, finely chopped |
| 1 sweet red pepper, seeded, deribbed, and finely chopped |
| 1 sweet green pepper, seeded, deribbed, and finely chopped |
| 8 garlic cloves, finely chopped |
| 6 large tomatoes, peeled, seeded, and chopped, or 28 oz. canned unsalted whole tomatoes, crushed and drained |
| ¼ cup finely chopped fresh oregano, or 4 tsp. dried oregano |
| 3 cups fresh breadcrumbs |
| 2 tbsp. currants (optional) |
| 20 canned grape leaves, stemmed, rinsed, and patted dry (optional) |

Heat a large, nonstick skillet over medium heat. Add the oil, carrots, celery, onions, eggplant, peppers, and garlic. Cook the mixture, stirring frequently, until the vegetables are soft—about eight minutes.

Add the tomatoes and oregano to the skillet. Increase the heat to medium high and bring the liquid to a simmer, then simmer the tomatoes for two minutes. Remove half of the mixture and set it aside.

Continue cooking the mixture in the skillet until the liquid has evaporated—about 10 minutes. Scrape the vegetables into a bowl and let them cool slightly. Add the beef, breadcrumbs, and currants, if you are using them. Knead the mixture to blend the ingredients.

Preheat the oven to 350° F. Line a 3-quart ring mold with the grape leaves, if you are using them. Spoon the meat mixture into the mold, patting it down gently to release trapped air. Trim any protruding grape leaves.

Bake the loaf for one hour. After about 50 minutes, reheat the reserved vegetable mixture over medium heat. Invert a serving plate on top of the mold; turn both over, then gently lift off the mold. Fill the space in the center of the meat loaf with some of the hot vegetables and spoon the rest into a bowl.

SUGGESTED ACCOMPANIMENT: *orzo or other small pasta.*

# Beef Tenderloin Roast with Spinach Sauce and Almonds

Serves 6
Working time: about 20 minutes
Total time: about 1 hour

| | |
|---|---|
| Calories **230** | one 1¾-lb. beef tenderloin roast, trimmed of fat |
| Protein **22g.** | 4 tsp. safflower oil |
| Cholesterol **64mg.** | ¼ tsp. salt |
| Total fat **13g.** | freshly ground black pepper |
| Saturated fat **3g.** | 2 tbsp. slivered almonds |
| Sodium **165mg.** | 3 tbsp. finely chopped shallots |
| | 1 cup dry white wine |
| | ½ lb. spinach, stemmed and washed |
| | ¼ cup skim milk |
| | ⅛ tsp. freshly grated or ground nutmeg |

Preheat the oven to 325° F.

Heat 1 teaspoon of the oil in a large, nonstick skillet over high heat. Sear the meat in the skillet until it is browned on all sides—two to three minutes in all. Season the tenderloin with ⅛ teaspoon of the salt and a liberal grinding of pepper. Transfer the tenderloin to a roasting pan; do not wash the skillet. Finish cooking the meat in the oven—about 35 minutes, or until a meat thermometer inserted in the center registers 140° F. for medium-rare meat.

Heat a small, heavy-bottomed skillet over medium heat. Add the slivered almonds and toast them, stirring constantly, until they are lightly browned—two to three minutes. Remove the toasted almonds from the skillet and set them aside.

To make the sauce, heat the remaining tablespoon of oil in the large skillet over medium heat. Add the shallots and cook them until they are translucent—about two minutes. Pour in the wine and simmer the liquid until about ⅓ cup remains—six to eight minutes.

Remove the roast from the oven and let it rest for 10 minutes while you complete the sauce.

Add the spinach to the shallot-wine mixture and reduce the heat to low. Cover the pan and cook the spinach until it has wilted—one to two minutes. Stir in the milk and nutmeg. Return the mixture to a simmer, then transfer it to a blender or a food processor and purée it. Season the sauce with the remaining ⅛ teaspoon of salt and some pepper.

Carve the tenderloin into 12 slices and arrange them on a warmed serving platter. Spoon some of the sauce over the slices and sprinkle them with the almonds. Pass the remaining sauce separately.

SUGGESTED ACCOMPANIMENT: *steamed julienned carrots.*

# Roast Eye Round with Mushroom Sauce

Serves 10
Working time: about 30 minutes
Total time: about 1 hour

Calories **205**
Protein **21g.**
Cholesterol **56mg.**
Total fat **10g.**
Saturated fat **3g.**
Sodium **170mg.**

| |
| --- |
| one 2½-lb. eye round roast, trimmed of fat |
| ¼ cup cracked black peppercorns |
| 2½ tbsp. Dijon mustard |
| 2 tbsp. plain low-fat yogurt |
| **Mushroom sauce** |
| 2 tbsp. virgin olive oil |
| ½ lb. mushrooms, wiped clean and quartered |
| ⅓ cup thinly sliced shallots |
| 1 tbsp. chopped fresh rosemary, or ¾ tsp. dried rosemary |
| 1 cup red wine |
| 1 garlic clove, finely chopped |
| 2 cups unsalted brown stock or unsalted chicken stock (recipes, page 138) |
| ¼ tsp. salt |
| ¼ cup heavy cream, mixed with 1 tbsp. cornstarch |

Preheat the oven to 500° F. Spread the cracked peppercorns on a plate. Mix 2 tablespoons of the mustard with the yogurt and spread this mixture all over the beef. Roll the beef in the cracked peppercorns, coating it evenly on all sides. Place the beef on a rack set in a roasting pan. For medium-rare meat, cook the roast until a meat thermometer inserted in the center registers 140° F.—about 35 minutes. Let the roast stand while you prepare the mushroom sauce.

Heat the olive oil in a large, heavy-bottomed, non-reactive skillet over medium heat. Add the mushrooms, shallots, and rosemary, and cook them, stirring often, for five minutes.

Add the wine and garlic to the skillet, then rapidly boil the liquid until it is reduced by half—about three minutes. Stir in the stock and salt; reduce the sauce once again until only about 1¼ cups of liquid remain. Whisk in the cream and cornstarch mixture along with the remaining ½ tablespoon of mustard; simmer the sauce for one minute more to thicken it.

To serve, carve the roast into 20 very thin slices. Arrange the slices on a platter and pour the mushroom sauce over them.

SUGGESTED ACCOMPANIMENT: *steamed broccoli florets.*

## Beef Tenderloin Roast with Spinach and Sprouts

Serves 8
Working time: about 30 minutes
Total time: about 2 hours (includes marinating)

Calories **240**
Protein **27g.**
Cholesterol **73mg.**
Total fat **12g.**
Saturated fat **4g.**
Sodium **160mg.**

| |
| --- |
| *one 2½-lb. beef tenderloin roast, trimmed of fat* |
| *2 tbsp. toasted sesame seeds* |
| *4 tbsp. low-sodium soy sauce* |
| *3 tbsp. rice vinegar or white wine vinegar* |
| *1 tbsp. dark brown sugar* |
| *1 tbsp. safflower oil* |
| *¾ lb. spinach, washed, stemmed, and sliced into ¼-inch-wide strips* |
| *2 large ripe tomatoes, peeled, seeded, and sliced into ¼-inch-wide strips* |
| *4 cups bean sprouts* |

To make the marinade, purée 1 tablespoon of the sesame seeds, 3 tablespoons of the soy sauce, 2 tablespoons of the vinegar, and the brown sugar in a blender. Put the tenderloin into a shallow, nonreactive dish, pour the marinade over it, and let it stand for one hour at room temperature, turning the meat occasionally.

Preheat the oven to 325° F. Drain the tenderloin, discarding the marinade, and pat it dry with paper towels. Pour the oil into a large, ovenproof skillet set over high heat. When the oil is hot, sear the meat until it is well browned on all sides—three to five minutes. Place the skillet in the oven. For medium-rare meat, roast the tenderloin for 40 to 45 minutes or until a meat thermometer inserted in the center registers 140° F. Remove the meat from the oven and let it rest while you prepare the garnish.

Heat a large skillet or wok over medium heat. Add the spinach strips and cook them, stirring constantly, until their liquid has evaporated—two to three minutes. Stir in the tomatoes and sprouts, and cook the vegetables until they are heated through—three to four minutes more. Remove the pan from the heat, and stir in the remaining tablespoon of soy sauce and the remaining tablespoon of vinegar.

Cut the tenderloin into 16 slices and arrange them on a platter. Surround the beef slices with the spinach, tomatoes, and sprouts. Sprinkle the remaining tablespoon of sesame seeds over the vegetables and serve.

SUGGESTED ACCOMPANIMENT: *boiled potatoes tossed with finely chopped scallion greens.*

## Beef Tenderloin Filled with Basil and Sun-Dried Tomatoes

Serves 4
Working time: about 35 minutes
Total time: about 2 hours

Calories **340**
Protein **28g.**
Cholesterol **74mg.**
Total fat **17g.**
Saturated fat **4g.**
Sodium **415mg.**

| |
| --- |
| one 1¼-lb. beef tenderloin roast, trimmed of fat |
| 1 cup loosely packed fresh basil leaves, thinly sliced, plus basil sprigs for garnish |
| ¼ cup sun-dried tomatoes packed in oil, drained and finely chopped |
| 1 tsp. safflower oil |

| Stuffed cherry tomatoes |
| --- |
| 2 whole garlic bulbs, the cloves separated but not peeled |
| 1 cup loosely packed fresh basil leaves |
| ⅛ tsp. salt |
| freshly ground black pepper |
| 1 tsp. fresh lemon juice |
| ¼ cup plain low-fat yogurt |
| 24 cherry tomatoes |

Preheat the oven to 325° F.

Using a well-scrubbed sharpening steel or some other thick, pointed tool, pierce the tenderloin through the center; rotate the sharpening steel to create a ½-inch-wide hole.

Combine the thinly sliced basil leaves with the sun-dried tomatoes. Using your hands, fill the tenderloin with the basil-tomato mixture.

Heat the oil in a heavy-bottomed, ovenproof skillet over high heat. When the oil is hot, sear the roast until it is well browned on all sides—three to five minutes. Transfer the skillet to the oven. For medium-rare meat, roast the tenderloin for 25 to 30 minutes, or until a thermometer inserted in the meat registers 140° F. Remove the tenderloin from the oven and let it rest until it is cool—about 45 minutes.

Meanwhile, prepare the filling for the cherry tomatoes. Put the garlic cloves into a small saucepan and pour in just enough water to cover them. Bring the water to a boil, then reduce the heat and simmer the cloves until they are very soft—30 to 45 minutes. Drain the garlic; when the cloves are cool enough to handle, squeeze the pulp from the skins into a blender or a food processor. Add the unsliced basil leaves, the salt, some pepper, the lemon juice, and the yogurt, and purée the mixture. Set the purée aside.

Cut the tops off the cherry tomatoes. With a melon baller or a small spoon, scoop out the seeds. Using a pastry bag or a spoon, fill the tomatoes with the purée.

Carve the tenderloin into ¼-inch-thick slices, and transfer them to individual plates or a platter. Arrange the filled tomatoes around the slices of tenderloin and serve the meat at room temperature, garnished with the sprigs of basil.

SUGGESTED ACCOMPANIMENT: *whole-wheat dinner rolls.*

# Roast Beef with Cloves and Red Peppers

Serves 12
Working time: about 30 minutes
Total time: about 2 hours

Calories **180**
Protein **23g.**
Cholesterol **63mg.**
Total fat **7g.**
Saturated fat **2g.**
Sodium **155mg.**

| |
|---|
| one 3½-lb. tip roast, trimmed of fat |
| 4 sweet red peppers |
| 1 tsp. ground cloves |
| 1 tbsp. safflower oil |
| ½ tsp. salt |
| freshly ground black pepper |
| 2 white onions (about 1 lb.) |
| 1 cup unsalted brown stock or unsalted chicken stock (recipes, page 138) |
| ½ cup dry white wine |

Roast the sweet peppers about 2 inches below a preheated broiler, turning them as their skins blister, until they are blackened on all sides—about 15 minutes in all. Transfer the peppers to a bowl and cover it with plastic wrap; the trapped steam will loosen their skins. Set the bowl aside.

Preheat the oven to 275° F. Sprinkle the meat all over with ½ teaspoon of the cloves.

Heat the oil in a large, heavy-bottomed skillet over high heat. When it is hot, add the beef and sear it until it is well browned on all sides—about five minutes. Transfer the beef to a shallow, flameproof casserole, and sprinkle it with ¼ teaspoon of the salt and a generous grinding of pepper.

Roast the beef for one hour. If the meat juices begin to blacken in the bottom of the casserole, pour in a few tablespoons of the stock.

While the roast is cooking, peel the peppers, working over a bowl to catch the juice. Strain the juice and set it aside. Slice the peppers into strips about 1 inch long and ½ inch wide. Cut the onions in half from top to bottom, then slice them with the grain into strips roughly the same size as the pepper strips.

When the roast has cooked for one hour, add to the casserole the peppers and their juice, the onions, the stock, the wine, the remaining ½ teaspoon of cloves, and the remaining ¼ teaspoon of salt. For medium-rare meat, cook the beef for 30 minutes longer, or until a meat thermometer inserted in the center of the roast registers 140° F.

Remove the casserole from the oven and set the roast aside while you finish preparing the dish.

With a slotted spoon, transfer the vegetables to a bowl. Boil the liquid remaining in the casserole until it is reduced to about ½ cup. Cut the meat into very thin slices and arrange them on a platter with the vegetables surrounding them. Drizzle the sauce over the beef and serve immediately.

SUGGESTED ACCOMPANIMENT: *roasted sweet potatoes.*

# Mushroom-Stuffed Top Loin Roast

Serves 8
Working time: about 45 minutes
Total time: about 2 hours

Calories **190**
Protein **26g.**
Cholesterol **65mg.**
Total fat **7g.**
Saturated fat **3g.**
Sodium **200mg.**

| |
|---|
| one 2½-lb. top loin roast, trimmed of fat |
| ½ lb. fresh shiitake mushrooms, wiped clean, caps finely chopped, stems reserved |
| ½ lb. mushrooms, wiped clean, caps finely chopped, stems reserved |

| |
|---|
| 2½ cups dry white wine |
| ½ cup Madeira or port |
| 8 scallions, white parts finely chopped, green parts reserved |
| grated zest of 3 lemons |
| ½ tsp. salt |
| freshly ground black pepper |
| ¼ cup toasted breadcrumbs |

Preheat the oven to 400° F.

Combine the mushroom caps, 2 cups of the white wine, and the Madeira or port in a large, nonreactive skillet. Bring the liquid to a boil over medium-high heat, then continue cooking it until all the liquid has evaporated—about 15 minutes. Transfer the mushrooms to a bowl and mix in the chopped scallions, lemon zest, salt, and some freshly ground black pepper. Set the mixture aside.

Using the techniques shown below, trim the fat from the roast, slice it, and stuff it. Put the roast into a roasting pan and cover the exposed mushroom mixture with the breadcrumbs. Scatter the reserved mushroom stems and scallion tops around the meat, and roast it for 30 minutes.

Pour the remaining ½ cup of white wine over the roast and continue roasting the beef for 15 minutes for medium-rare meat. (The internal temperature should be 140° F.) Transfer the roast to a cutting board and allow it to rest for 15 minutes.

Heat the juices in the roasting pan over medium heat, scraping up any caramelized juices with a wooden spoon to dissolve them. Skim off the fat, strain the juices, and keep them warm.

Carve the roast into eight slices and serve them with the juices spooned on top.

SUGGESTED ACCOMPANIMENT: *steamed spinach.*

EDITOR'S NOTE: *If fresh shiitake mushrooms are unavailable, regular mushrooms may be substituted.*

## Stuffing a Top Loin Roast

1 TRIMMING THE FAT. *With a small, thin-bladed knife, cut into the fatty layer of the roast to form a tab. Pull the tab taut, and insert the knife under it. Carefully slide the knife toward you to remove a strip of fat. Continue cutting off strips until all the fat is removed.*

2 MAKING THE FIRST SLICE. *Steadying the roast with one hand, place a slicing knife along the meat's edge, about one-third of the way down from the surface. With a smooth sawing motion, cut across the meat, stopping just short of the edge so that the flaps remain attached.*

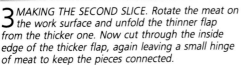

3 MAKING THE SECOND SLICE. *Rotate the meat on the work surface and unfold the thinner flap from the thicker one. Now cut through the inside edge of the thicker flap, again leaving a small hinge of meat to keep the pieces connected.*

4 STUFFING THE LOIN. *Unfold the newly formed flap. You will have three joined squares of meat. Spread one-third of the stuffing onto the middle square and fold the left flap over it. Spread half of the remaining stuffing on top (above). Fold the right flap over the stuffing and cover the flap with the rest of the stuffing.*

# French-Roasted Veal with Grapefruit and Herbs

COOKING LARGE PIECES OF MEAT AND WHOLE BIRDS IN A
SMALL AMOUNT OF LIQUID IS CALLED FRENCH ROASTING AND IS
A GOOD WAY TO ROAST LEAN MEATS TO ENSURE SUCCULENCE.
WHEN ROASTED WITHOUT LIQUID, LEAN CUTS TEND TO
TOUGHEN AND DRY OUT.

Serves 6
Working time: about 40 minutes
Total time: about 1 hour and 20 minutes

Calories **250**
Protein **15g.**
Cholesterol **120mg.**
Total fat **13g.**
Saturated fat **5g.**
Sodium **155mg.**

| |
| --- |
| one 2½- to 3-lb. veal loin roast, boned and trimmed of fat |
| 3 grapefruits |
| 1 garlic clove, crushed |
| 2 tbsp. grainy mustard |
| 2 tsp. chopped fresh rosemary, or 1 tsp. dried rosemary, crumbled |
| 2 tsp. chopped fresh thyme, or ½ tsp. dried thyme leaves |
| freshly ground black pepper |
| 1 tbsp. virgin olive oil |
| 1 cup unsalted chicken stock or unsalted veal stock (recipes, page 138) |
| 1 bouquet garni (parsley, thyme, bay leaf) |
| ⅛ tsp. salt |
| rosemary and thyme sprigs for garnish (optional) |

Preheat the oven to 350° F.

Finely grate the zest of two of the grapefruits into a bowl. Add the crushed garlic, then half each of the mustard, chopped rosemary, chopped thyme, and some freshly ground black pepper. Mix the ingredients well, then spread over the inside (boned-out part) of the veal. Roll up the roast and tie it securely at regular intervals with string.

Halve one of the three grapefruits and squeeze the juice. Heat the oil in a large, flameproof casserole over high heat and sear the veal on all sides, turning it frequently—about 10 minutes in all. Spread the remaining tablespoon of mustard over the outside of the seared veal. Pour the grapefruit juice and the stock over the veal, and bring the liquid to a boil. Add the bouquet garni, the salt, and some pepper. Transfer the casserole to the oven and roast, uncovered, for 30 minutes, turning the veal over every 10 minutes or so and basting with the cooking juices. The meat is ready if the juices run clear when a skewer is inserted in the center of the roast—or the internal temperature reading is 145° F. on a meat thermometer. While the veal is cooking, peel and segment the remaining two grapefruits for the garnish. Prepare the grapefruit segments over a bowl to catch the juice, and set both segments and juice aside.

Transfer the roast veal to a warmed serving dish, cover it, and keep it hot. Place the casserole on top of the stove and remove the bouquet garni. Add the grapefruit juice from the garnish to the cooking juices and boil the liquid to reduce it slightly, stirring con-

tinuously—about five minutes. Remove the casserole from the heat and stir in the remaining chopped herbs.

Remove the string from the veal and carve the meat into neat slices. Arrange them on a platter or individual plates with the grapefruit segments. Pour over a little of the cooking juices, and garnish with sprigs of rosemary and thyme, if desired. Pass the remaining cooking juices separately.

SUGGESTED ACCOMPANIMENT: *steamed broccoli and new potatoes.*

EDITOR'S NOTE: *To give this dish added color, use segments of one pink and one yellow-fleshed grapefruit for the garnish.*

# Peppered Loin of Veal

Serves 4
Working time: about 20 minutes
Total time: about 3 hours (includes marinating)

Calories **180**
Protein **40g.**
Cholesterol **90mg.**
Total fat **10g.**
Saturated fat **2g.**
Sodium **185mg.**

| |
|---|
| one 1-lb. piece loin of veal, trimmed of fat |
| 2½ tbsp. pumpkin seeds |
| 1 tsp. dried green peppercorns |
| ½ tsp. black peppercorns |
| ¼ tsp. hot red-pepper flakes |
| 1 tsp. Dijon mustard |
| ¾ lb. ripe tomatoes, peeled, seeded, and chopped, or 1 cup canned tomatoes, drained and chopped |
| watercress sprigs for garnish |

Toast the pumpkin seeds in a small, nonstick skillet over medium heat, until they are golden brown but not too brown—stirring them with a long-handled spoon and standing well back because the seeds will snap and jump. Grind the toasted seeds finely in a blender or food processor.

Crush the green and black peppercorns and the pepper flakes finely with a mortar and pestle, then turn them into a medium-size bowl. Add the pumpkin seeds and the mustard, mix well, then add the tomatoes and bind the ingredients to a wet paste. Place the loin of veal in the bowl and spread the paste all over it. Cover and marinate the veal in the refrigerator for at least two hours.

Preheat the oven to 475° F.

Transfer the veal to a small roasting pan and press on any pepper paste left in the bowl, taking care to see that the ends are also covered. Roast for 10 minutes, then lower the heat to 350° F. and continue roasting for 15 minutes longer. The veal should still be pink at this point; if you prefer the meat well done, roast for 10 to 15 minutes more.

Remove the veal from the oven, cover it loosely with foil, and let it rest in a warm place for 10 minutes. To serve, carve the veal into thick slices and garnish with watercress sprigs.

SUGGESTED ACCOMPANIMENT: *steamed, buttered pumpkin and snow peas.*

## Roast Loin of Veal with Corn and Watercress Pilaf

Serves 8
Working time: about 1 hour
Total time: about 2 hours

Calories **275**
Protein **30g.**
Cholesterol **110mg.**
Total fat **14g.**
Saturated fat **5g.**
Sodium **220mg.**

| |
|---|
| 2 lb. boned veal loin roast |
| 2 tsp. safflower oil |
| 1 onion, finely chopped |
| 1 celery stalk, finely chopped |
| 2 tbsp. low-fat milk |
| ¾ cup cooked brown rice |
| 10 oz. fresh corn kernels (about 4 ears), or 10 oz. frozen corn, thawed and drained |
| 2 cups loosely packed watercress leaves, chopped |
| ½ tsp. salt |
| freshly ground black pepper |
| ¼ cup medium-dry sherry |

Trim any excess fat from the veal loin roast, being careful not to cut through the membranes that hold the veal together. Open out the roast on a work surface.

Preheat the oven to 350° F. Heat the oil in a small, nonstick skillet over medium-low heat. Add the chopped onion and celery, and cook them gently, stirring, until they are softened—about five minutes. Transfer the vegetables to a bowl.

Put the milk into a food processor and add a quarter of the rice. Blend the milk and rice to a smooth paste, then turn the paste into a bowl.

Add the corn to the onion and celery together with the watercress, the salt, and some pepper, and mix the ingredients together. Add a quarter of this mixture to the rice paste and mix well. Spread the corn and rice paste over the surface of the veal, then roll it up and tie it with string *(page 135, Step 3)*. Put the veal into a roasting bag and place the bag in a roasting pan.

Add the remaining rice to the rest of the corn mixture and spoon it into the roasting bag around the veal. Close the end of the bag with string, and cut several slits in the bag. Roast for one hour. Test if the veal is cooked by piercing it with a skewer or the tip of a knife through one of the slits in the bag: The juices that run out of the meat should be only faintly pink, or clear.

Cut open the top of the roasting bag and lift the veal onto a carving board. Use a slotted spoon to transfer the corn and watercress pilaf to a serving platter, being sure to drain the pilaf well. Cover the roast and the pilaf and set them aside to rest in a warm place for 10 minutes. While the meat is resting, strain the cooking juices left in the roasting bag into a small, nonreactive saucepan. Add the sherry, bring to a boil, and boil for one minute.

Cut the veal roast into thick slices and arrange the slices over the bed of pilaf on the serving platter. Drizzle the sherried juices over the sliced veal and serve the dish immediately.

SUGGESTED ACCOMPANIMENTS: *whole-grain bread; carrots.*

# Veal Chops with Artichokes

Serves 4
Working time: about 45 minutes
Total time: about 1 hour and 45 minutes

Calories **280**
Protein **24g.**
Cholesterol **120mg.**
Total fat **17g.**
Saturated fat **6g.**
Sodium **315mg.**

| |
|---|
| 4 veal loin chops (about ½ lb. each), trimmed of fat |
| ¼ cup lemon juice |
| 4 large artichokes, thoroughly washed |
| 1 tbsp. safflower oil |
| ¼ cup dry sherry |
| 1½ tbsp. chopped fresh tarragon or oregano, or 1 tsp. dried oregano plus some chopped fresh parsley |
| ½ tsp. salt |
| freshly ground black pepper |
| 2 tbsp. heavy cream |

Bring about 2 quarts of water to a boil in a large, nonreactive pan. Add the lemon juice. Cut off the stems of the artichokes close to the bottom and place them bottom down in the boiling water. (This will seal the cut surface and keep it from discoloring.) Simmer the artichokes for about 30 minutes. To test if they are cooked, insert a knife in an artichoke bottom. It should meet no resistance, and a leaf gently tugged should easily pull free. Drain the artichokes by putting them upside down in a colander.

Preheat the oven to 350° F. When the artichokes are cool enough to handle, pull off and reserve the leaves; discard the choke. Trim the artichoke bottoms into neat rounds, reserving the trimmings. Cut the bottoms into ¼-inch cubes.

Heat the oil in a large, nonstick skillet over high heat. Add the chops and brown them for one to two minutes on each side. Transfer the chops to a large sheet of foil placed on a baking sheet. Pile the diced artichoke bottoms on the chops, then sprinkle the sherry, two-thirds of the tarragon or fresh oregano (or all of the dried oregano, if you are using it), the salt, and some pepper on the chops. Wrap the foil around the chops and seal it tightly. Put the chops into the oven and bake them for 15 minutes.

Meanwhile, scrape off the tender, bottom part of each artichoke leaf, and put it into a food processor or blender with the trimmings; discard the leaves.

Carefully transfer the chops to a serving platter and keep them hot. To make the sauce, pour the cooking juices from the foil into the food processor or blender, and purée the artichoke mixture with the juices. Pass the mixture through a fine sieve into a small saucepan and add the cream. Bring to a boil and boil for one minute. Spoon the sauce around the chops, sprinkle with the remaining fresh herbs (or a little parsley, if dried oregano has been used), and serve immediately.

SUGGESTED ACCOMPANIMENTS: *baked potatoes; red onion and fennel salad.*

# Loin of Veal Stuffed with Oranges and Black Olives

Serves 4
Working time: about 35 minutes
Total time: about 1 hour and 10 minutes

Calories **400**
Protein **30g.**
Cholesterol **90mg.**
Total fat **9g.**
Saturated fat **2g.**
Sodium **240mg.**

| |
| --- |
| one 1-lb. piece loin of veal, trimmed of fat |
| 3 oranges |
| 6 black olives, pitted and chopped |
| 6 tbsp. fresh whole-wheat breadcrumbs |
| 1 egg white |
| freshly ground black pepper |
| 2 garlic cloves, cut into thin slivers |
| 1 tbsp. virgin olive oil |
| 1 tbsp. brandy |
| 2 tbsp. dry white wine |
| ¾ cup freshly squeezed orange juice |
| 3 bay leaves |
| black olives for garnish |

Preheat the oven to 350° F. Grate the zest of two of the oranges. Remove the peel and pith of all three oranges, then chop the flesh of one and slice the other two, halving each slice.

Cut a slit along one side of the veal to make a pocket in the center. Put the orange zest and the chopped orange into a bowl, and add the olives, breadcrumbs, egg white, and some pepper. Stir well to mix. Pack the stuffing mixture into the pocket in the veal, close up the slit, and tie the loin neatly into shape with string *(page 135, Step 3)*. Make small incisions in the meat at regular intervals with the point of a sharp knife, then insert the garlic. Rub a little pepper all over the meat.

Heat the oil in a flameproof casserole over high heat. Add the veal and sear it on all sides—about five minutes. Remove the casserole and lower the heat.

Warm the brandy gently in a ladle. Remove it from the heat, light it with a match, and pour the flaming brandy over the veal. When the flames subside, pour over the white wine and orange juice. Return the casserole to the heat and bring the liquid slowly to a boil. Add the bay leaves. Transfer the casserole to the oven and roast the veal, uncovered, for 30 minutes, turning the veal over and basting it with the cooking juices about every 10 minutes.

Transfer the meat to a warmed serving dish, cover it, and keep it hot. Place the casserole on top of the stove and discard the bay leaves. Boil to reduce slightly, stirring all the time—three to five minutes.

Remove the string from the veal and carve the meat into neat slices. Arrange the veal and orange slices attractively on a warmed serving platter. Pour a little of the cooking juices over them, and garnish the dish with the black olives. Serve immediately.

SUGGESTED ACCOMPANIMENT: *green beans.*

# Veal Chops with Spinach and Ricotta

Serves 4
Working time: about 45 minutes
Total time: about 1 hour and 15 minutes

Calories **310**
Protein **33g.**
Cholesterol **120mg.**
Total fat **17g.**
Saturated fat **5g.**
Sodium **290mg.**

| |
|---|
| 4 veal loin chops (about ½ lb. each), trimmed of fat |
| 1½ lb. ripe tomatoes (about 4), peeled, seeded, and chopped, or 14 oz. canned tomatoes, chopped |
| 2 large sprigs fresh rosemary, or 1 tsp. dried rosemary, crumbled |
| 2 tbsp. virgin olive oil |
| 1 onion, finely chopped |
| 3 cups spinach leaves, washed, drained, and chopped |
| ⅓ cup low-fat ricotta cheese |
| ⅛ tsp. freshly grated or ground nutmeg |
| ¼ tsp. salt |
| freshly ground black pepper |
| 1 garlic clove, crushed |
| small rosemary sprigs for garnish (optional) |

Cut a pocket in the meaty part of each chop, through to the bone (or ask the butcher to do this for you). Set the chops aside. Put the tomatoes into a heavy-bottomed, nonreactive saucepan with the rosemary,

adding a little water if you are using fresh tomatoes. Simmer for 10 minutes, stirring occasionally.

Meanwhile, heat 1 tablespoon of the oil in a large, nonstick skillet over low heat. Add the onion and cook gently, stirring occasionally, until it is softened—about five minutes. Add the chopped spinach and cook, stirring, until it has wilted and the excess moisture has evaporated—three to four minutes.

Transfer the spinach mixture to a bowl. Add half of the ricotta, all of the nutmeg, the salt, and some pepper to the spinach, mix well, and set aside.

Preheat the oven to 350° F. Combine the garlic with the remaining ricotta; divide the mixture into four portions and use it to stuff the pockets in the chops. Close the openings with wooden toothpicks.

Heat the remaining oil in a large, nonstick skillet over medium-high heat and brown the chops on both sides—about five minutes in all. Transfer the chops to a baking dish in which they fit comfortably side by side (above). Spread the spinach and ricotta mixture over them. Discard the rosemary sprigs, if you are using them, from the tomatoes, and spoon the tomatoes over the chops to cover the cheese mixture. Bake for 30 minutes. Remove the toothpicks and serve the chops hot, garnished, if you like, with rosemary sprigs.

SUGGESTED ACCOMPANIMENT: *risotto with eggplant and sweet red pepper.*

2 *Tropical fruit provides a refreshing garnish for spicy pan-fried sirloin steaks (recipe, page 69).*

# Quick Sautés and Stir-Fries

Sautéing and stir-frying are techniques with a great deal in common. Both involve cooking food in a pan, in a little fat, over direct heat. The only difference between the two techniques is the type of pan used.

Traditionally, sautéing employs a heavy-bottomed sauté pan. Nowadays, some cooks prefer to use a lighter, nonstick skillet. But, basically, the shape of the pan is the same—shallow, with a wide, flat bottom. It is the style of vessel adopted by Western cuisines, and its name, "sauté," is derived from the French *sauter,* meaning to jump. Professional cooks make the food literally jump with a flick of the hand grasping the pan's handle: The less skilled can prevent burning and sticking equally well by stirring and turning.

The cousin of the sauté pan used in China and Southeast Asia is the wok. With its small well and its tall, curved sides, the wok permits finely sliced or shredded food to be stirred and tossed vigorously without danger of its flying out of the pan.

With both sautéing and stir-frying a small amount of oil or fat is used to cook the meat in the preliminary stage; during this time, a fairly high heat is used to seal in the meat's juices and brown the surface. The two techniques are, therefore, essentially dry-cooking methods, even though many sautés and stir-fries introduce a liquid of some kind at a later stage. Table wine, fortified wine, stock, sake, soy sauce, vinegar, tomato purée, and fruit juices can all enhance beef and veal dishes. Another valuable addition is a marinade in which the food has been steeped, as with the stir-fried ginger beef with watercress on page 73.

For the health-conscious cook, the wok offers an advantage during the preliminary browning process: It minimizes the amount of fat or oil needed. The oil collects in the compact well, so that a small volume supplies a sufficient depth to cook the food. But a wok has its limitations. It is not suitable for cooking large pieces of meat, such as whole veal cutlets. These must be browned in a sauté pan, so that the slices can be arranged in a single layer without overlapping.

The sauté pan is also indispensable for those dishes where a sauce is created by rapid reduction of the liquid—thus eliminating the need for the thickenings of cream or of butter and flour that appeared in so many old-fashioned beef and veal recipes. The sauté pan's wide, flat bottom permits a large volume of liquid to boil down quickly into an intensely flavored sauce. In the medallions of veal with rosemary *(page 78),* for example, stock and red wine are concentrated to make a sauce of rich flavor and velvety texture that needs no additional thickening. The other recipes in this chapter offer equally delicious adaptations of traditions from East and West.

## Stir-Fried Beef with Pine Nuts on Nappa Cabbage

Serves 4
Working (and total) time: about 20 minutes

Calories **225**
Protein **19g.**
Cholesterol **54mg.**
Total fat **13g.**
Saturated fat **3g.**
Sodium **165mg.**

|  |
| --- |
| 1 lb. beef tenderloin, trimmed of fat and cut into thin strips |
| 4 tsp. cornstarch |
| freshly ground black pepper |
| 1 tsp. oyster sauce |
| 1 tsp. low-sodium soy sauce |
| 1 tbsp. dry sherry |
| ½ tsp. sugar |
| 1½ tbsp. safflower oil |
| ⅓ cup finely chopped onion |
| ½ sweet green pepper, seeded, deribbed, and finely chopped |
| 1 celery stalk, finely chopped |
| 1 scallion, trimmed and thinly sliced |
| 8 Nappa cabbage leaves or iceberg lettuce leaves, washed and dried |
| 2 tbsp. pine nuts |

Put the beef strips into a bowl, and sprinkle them with 2 teaspoons of the cornstarch and the pepper. Toss the strips to coat them and let them stand at room tem-perature while you prepare the remaining ingredients.

In a small bowl, combine the remaining 2 teaspoons of cornstarch, the oyster sauce, the soy sauce, the sherry, and the sugar. Set the bowl aside.

Heat the oil in a large, nonstick skillet or a well-seasoned wok over high heat. When the oil is hot, add the beef strips and stir-fry them until the meat lightens in color but is still slightly pink—one to two minutes. Use a slotted spoon to transfer the meat to a plate; set the plate aside.

Return the skillet or wok to high heat. Add the onion, green pepper, and celery, and stir-fry them for 30 seconds. Return the meat to the pan, then cook the mixture, stirring continuously, until it is hot—10 to 15 seconds. Pour the oyster-sauce mixture over the in-gredients in the pan. Stir-fry the meat and vegetables until the sauce thickens and coats them—30 seconds to one minute. Remove the pan from the heat.

Toss the scallion with the beef and vegetables. Set two cabbage or lettuce leaves on each plate; divide the mixture among the leaves. Sprinkle the pine nuts over the beef and vegetables and serve immediately.

---

SUGGESTED ACCOMPANIMENT: *a salad of rice noodles and shredded carrots.*

EDITOR'S NOTE: *If oyster sauce is not available, you may sub-stitute an additional teaspoon of low-sodium soy sauce.*

# Top Round Sautéed with Broccoli

Serves 6
Working (and total) time: about 40 minutes

Calories **250**
Protein **27g.**
Cholesterol **60mg.**
Total fat **11g.**
Saturated fat **3g.**
Sodium **355mg.**

| |
|---|
| 1½ lb. top round steak, trimmed of fat and cut into very thin strips about 1½ inches long |
| 1½ tsp. chili paste, or ½ tsp. hot red-pepper flakes |
| 4 garlic cloves, very finely chopped |
| 1½ cups unsalted brown stock or unsalted chicken stock (recipes, page 138) |
| 1 tbsp. cornstarch |
| 1 lb. broccoli, the stalks peeled and cut into thin strips about 1½ inches long, the tops cut into small florets |
| 1¼ lb. cauliflower (about ½ large head), cut into small florets |
| 2 tbsp. safflower oil |
| ½ tsp. salt |
| 2 lemons, peeled and cut into ½-inch pieces |

Put the steak strips into a bowl with the chili paste or hot red-pepper flakes and the garlic, and let them marinate while you prepare the other ingredients.

Pour the stock into a small saucepan and boil it until about ⅔ cup remains. In a small bowl, mix 2 tablespoons of the reduced stock with the cornstarch.

Blanch the broccoli and cauliflower together in 3 quarts of boiling water for one minute. Drain the vegetables, refresh them under cold running water, and drain them again.

Heat 1 tablespoon of the safflower oil in a large, nonstick skillet or a well-seasoned wok over high heat. When the oil is hot, add the vegetables, sprinkle them with the salt, and sauté the mixture for two minutes. With a slotted spoon, transfer the cooked vegetables to a serving bowl.

Pour the remaining tablespoon of oil into the skillet or wok. Add the marinated steak strips and sauté them until they are lightly browned—about one minute.

Return the vegetables to the skillet or wok. Pour in the cornstarch mixture and the remaining stock, then add half of the lemon pieces. Cook the mixture, stirring, for a minute and a half, then use a slotted spoon to transfer it to a serving dish.

Boil the sauce remaining in the pan until it is reduced to about ½ cup, and pour it over the meat and vegetables. Scatter the remaining lemon pieces over the dish and serve it immediately.

# Beef and Wheat-Berry Salad

Serves 6
Working time: about 25 minutes
Total time: about 50 minutes

Calories **355**
Protein **29g.**
Cholesterol **63mg.**
Total fat **10g.**
Saturated fat **3g.**
Sodium **235mg.**

| |
|---|
| 1½ lb. boneless sirloin steak, trimmed of fat and cut into strips about 1½ inches long and ⅛ inch thick |
| 1½ cups wheat berries, rinsed |
| ½ tsp. salt |
| 2 leeks, trimmed, or 2 bunches scallions, trimmed |
| 1 tbsp. virgin olive oil |
| 2 tsp. chopped fresh thyme, or ¾ tsp. dried thyme leaves |
| 8 large radishes, quartered |
| ¼ cup cider vinegar |
| 1½ tbsp. fresh lemon juice |
| freshly ground black pepper |

Bring 2½ cups of water to a boil in a saucepan. Add the wheat berries and ¼ teaspoon of the salt. Reduce the heat to low and partially cover the pan. Simmer the wheat berries until they are just tender—about 45 minutes. Drain the wheat berries and set them aside.

Meanwhile, if you are using leeks, slice them into rounds about ½ inch wide. Wash the rounds in two or three changes of cold water to rid them of grit. Drain the rounds and set them aside. (If you are using scallions, simply slice them.)

Ten minutes before the wheat berries are ready, heat 2 teaspoons of the oil in a large, nonstick skillet over high heat. Add the beef and thyme, and cook them, stirring frequently, for two minutes; transfer the beef to a large bowl.

Return the skillet to the heat and add the remaining teaspoon of oil. Add the leeks or scallions and the radishes, and cook them, stirring frequently, for three minutes. Pour in the vinegar, the lemon juice, the reserved beef and wheat berries, the remaining ¼ teaspoon of salt, and a generous grinding of black pepper. Continue cooking, stirring frequently, for one additional minute. With a slotted spoon, transfer the mixture to a large serving bowl.

Return the skillet to high heat and boil the liquid until it is reduced to ¼ cup. Pour the reduced liquid over the salad and toss the ingredients well. Serve the salad warm or chilled.

SUGGESTED ACCOMPANIMENTS: *sliced fruit; French bread.*

## Beef Tenderloin Stir-Fried with Butternut Squash and Turnips

Serves 4
Working time: about 15 minutes
Total time: about 25 minutes

| | |
|---|---|
| Calories **215** | 1 lb. beef tenderloin, trimmed of fat and sliced into 2-inch-long strips |
| Protein **20g.** | |
| Cholesterol **54mg.** | 1¼ cups unsalted brown stock or unsalted chicken stock (recipes, page 138) |
| Total fat **10g.** | |
| Saturated fat **3g.** | 1 small onion, thinly sliced |
| Sodium **235mg.** | 2 turnips (about ½ lb.), peeled, quartered, and cut into ¼-inch-thick slices |
| | ½ small butternut squash (about ¾ lb.), peeled, quartered, and cut into ¼-inch-thick slices |
| | 2 tbsp. chopped fresh tarragon, or 2 tsp. dried tarragon |
| | ¼ tsp. salt |
| | freshly ground black pepper |
| | 1 tbsp. safflower oil |
| | 1 garlic clove, finely chopped |
| | 1 tbsp. cornstarch, mixed with 1 tbsp. water |
| | 1 tsp. distilled white vinegar |

Place the stock and the onion in a saucepan. Set a vegetable steamer in the pan and bring the stock to a simmer. In the meantime, sprinkle the turnips and the squash separately with 1 tablespoon of the fresh tarragon or all of the dried. Put the turnips into the steamer, cover it, and steam the turnips for two minutes. Add the squash and continue steaming the vegetables until they are tender—about three minutes. Transfer the vegetables to a plate and set them aside; remove the steamer from the saucepan, and reserve the stock and onion.

Season the beef with the salt and pepper. Heat ½ tablespoon of the oil in a well-seasoned wok or a heavy-bottomed skillet over high heat, and sear the beef, tossing continuously to prevent it from sticking, for about two minutes. Turn off the heat, transfer the meat to a plate, and keep it warm. Wipe out the wok or skillet with a paper towel, and set it over high heat again. Add the remaining ½ tablespoon of oil, the garlic, and the reserved turnips and squash, and cook them briefly, stirring continuously, for three minutes. Add the beef, toss well, and push the ingredients to the sides of the wok or skillet. Pour in the reserved stock and onions, and bring them to a simmer. Whisk in the cornstarch mixture and the vinegar, whisking continuously until the liquid thickens—about two minutes. Serve the beef and vegetables with the sauce. If you are using fresh tarragon, sprinkle the remaining tablespoon over the top.

SUGGESTED ACCOMPANIMENT: *rice tossed with chives.*

# Top Round Steak with Mushrooms and Red Onions

Serves 8
Working time: about 1 hour
Total time: about 3 hours (includes marinating time)

Calories **245**
Protein **29g.**
Cholesterol **72mg.**
Total fat **8g.**
Saturated fat **3g.**
Sodium **70mg.**

| |
|---|
| one 2½-lb. top round steak, trimmed of fat |
| 2 red onions, cut into ½-inch-thick slices |
| 1½ cups red wine |
| ¼ cup raspberry vinegar or distilled white vinegar |
| ¼ cup fresh lime juice |
| 20 juniper berries |
| 1 lb. mushrooms, wiped clean |
| ¾ cup unsalted brown stock or unsalted chicken stock (recipes, page 138) |
| 2 tbsp. cornstarch |
| freshly ground black pepper |
| ¼ cup finely chopped fresh parsley |

Spread the onion slices in the bottom of a shallow, nonreactive baking dish. Set the steak on the onions; pour the wine, vinegar, and lime juice over the steak, then scatter the juniper berries over all. Let the steak marinate at room temperature for two hours or put it into the refrigerator overnight.

Remove the steak and onions from the marinade, and pat them dry with paper towels. Strain the marinade into a bowl and set it aside. Discard the berries.

Heat a large, nonstick skillet over high heat. Add the onion slices and sauté them until they are tender—about four minutes on each side. Remove them from the skillet and keep them warm. Cook the steak in the skillet over medium-high heat for four minutes on each side for medium-rare meat. Remove the steak from the skillet and let it rest while you prepare the mushrooms.

Sauté the mushrooms in the skillet over high heat, stirring occasionally, until most of the juices have evaporated—about five minutes. Remove the mushrooms with a slotted spoon and set them aside. Pour the steak marinade into the skillet and boil it until it has reduced by half—about 10 minutes. Mix the stock and the cornstarch together, and whisk them into the reduced marinade. Bring the liquid to a boil and continue cooking until it thickens slightly—about one minute. Season the mushrooms with some black pepper and stir them, along with the parsley, into the sauce.

Slice the steak and arrange it on a serving platter with the onions. Spoon the mushrooms around the steak just before serving.

SUGGESTED ACCOMPANIMENT: *French bread.*

# Beef Stroganoff with Wild Mushrooms

Serves 4
Working time: about 40 minutes
Total time: about 1 hour

Calories **220**
Protein **24g.**
Cholesterol **50mg.**
Total fat **12g.**
Saturated fat **3g.**
Sodium **150mg.**

| |
|---|
| ¾ lb. beef tenderloin, trimmed of fat |
| ½ oz. dried ceps (porcini), or other dried wild mushrooms, soaked in ⅔ cup warm water for 20 minutes |
| 2 tbsp. virgin olive oil |
| 6 to 8 shallots, thinly sliced |
| ¼ lb. mushrooms, wiped clean and sliced |
| ½ tsp. dried green peppercorns, crushed |
| ¼ tsp. salt |
| 3 tbsp. sour cream |
| 2 tbsp. plain low-fat yogurt |
| ½ tsp. Dijon mustard |
| 2 firm ripe tomatoes, peeled, seeded, and cut into thin strips |
| 1 small pickled gherkin, cut into short thin strips |

Cut the beef tenderloin crosswise (against the grain) into slices about ¼ inch thick. Cut the slices into strips about 1½ inches long. Drain the soaked mushrooms, reserving the soaking water, and remove any remaining sand or grit under running water; then chop them coarsely. Strain the soaking water through a sieve lined with paper towels.

Heat 2 teaspoons of the oil in a large, nonstick skillet over medium heat. Add the shallots and cook for two minutes, stirring, then add the wild mushrooms, soaking water, and sliced mushrooms. Cook, stirring frequently, until the excess liquid has evaporated—about 10 minutes. Remove the mushroom mixture from the pan. Heat another 2 teaspoons of the oil in the pan over high heat and add half of the beef. Sauté briskly for three to four minutes, stirring and tossing to brown the strips evenly. Add the browned strips to the mushroom mixture. Heat the remaining oil in the pan and brown the remaining beef strips in the same way. Return the first batch of beef and the mushroom mixture to the pan and stir. Add the peppercorns and salt.

In a small bowl, stir together the sour cream, yogurt, and mustard. Add to the pan with the tomato strips and gherkin strips. Fold together gently but thoroughly, and heat without boiling. Serve hot.

SUGGESTED ACCOMPANIMENTS: *noodles; curly endive salad.*

# Steaks Creole

Serves 4
Working time: about 45 minutes
Total time: about 5 hours (includes marinating)

Calories **320**
Protein **29g.**
Cholesterol **60mg.**
Total fat **11g.**
Saturated fat **3g.**
Sodium **120mg.**

| |
|---|
| 1 lb. sirloin or top loin steaks, trimmed of fat, cut into four ¾-inch-thick pieces |
| ¾ lb. fresh pineapple, peeled and sliced crosswise |
| ¾ lb. watermelon, peeled and sliced |
| 1 papaya, peeled, halved, seeded, and sliced |
| 1 mango, peeled, pitted, and sliced |
| 1 tbsp. virgin olive oil |
| 2 tbsp. lime juice |
| 2 tsp. chopped fresh mint |
| ⅛ tsp. salt |
| **Rum marinade** |
| 2 tbsp. dark rum |
| ½ tbsp. virgin olive oil |
| 2 garlic cloves, crushed |
| 12 whole allspice, crushed |
| 1 tsp. cayenne pepper |

*freshly ground black pepper*

To make the marinade, mix together the rum, oil, garlic, whole allspice, cayenne pepper, and some black pepper. Put the beef into a shallow, nonreactive dish and brush the marinade over both sides of each steak. Cover the steaks loosely and let them marinate in a cold place or the refrigerator for at least four hours, preferably overnight.

Before cooking, let the steaks stand at room temperature for 30 minutes. Meanwhile, arrange the sliced fruit on individual plates. Whisk together the oil, lime juice, mint, and salt, and set aside.

Place the steaks in a heavy, nonstick skillet over high heat. Cook them for four minutes on each side for rare steaks, or longer if you prefer them well done. Arrange the steaks on the plates with the sliced fruit. Drizzle the dressing over the fruit or serve it separately. Serve the steaks at once.

EDITOR'S NOTE: *This dish is best served without additional accompaniments, which would mar the complementary flavors of meat and fruit.*

# Southeast Asian Beef Noodles

Serves 4
Working (and total) time: about 45 minutes

Calories **420**
Protein **33g.**
Cholesterol **72mg.**
Total fat **13g.**
Saturated fat **3g.**
Sodium **260mg.**

| |
|---|
| 1¼ lb. top round, trimmed of fat and cut into paper-thin slices |
| 1 tbsp. low-sodium soy sauce |
| 2 tbsp. dry sherry or dry white wine |
| 2 tbsp. sugar |
| freshly ground black pepper |
| 1½ tbsp. cornstarch |
| 6 oz. fresh Asian wheat noodles, such as udon noodles, or 4 oz. vermicelli |

| |
|---|
| 4 tsp. safflower oil |
| 1 small onion, halved and sliced lengthwise |
| 1 carrot, peeled, halved lengthwise, and thinly sliced on the diagonal |
| ½ lb. broccoli stems, peeled, halved lengthwise, and thinly sliced on the diagonal |
| ½ sweet red pepper, seeded, deribbed, and cut into narrow strips about 2 inches long |
| 2 tsp. finely chopped fresh ginger |
| 4 garlic cloves, finely chopped |
| 1 cup unsalted brown stock or unsalted chicken stock (recipes, page 138) |
| ½ tbsp. sweet chili sauce, or ½ tsp. hot-red-pepper flakes mixed with ½ tsp. corn syrup and ½ tsp. rice vinegar |
| 1 tbsp. fresh lemon juice |
| 1 tbsp. hoisin sauce or low-sodium soy sauce |

In a large bowl, combine the beef with the tablespoon of soy sauce, the sherry or white wine, 1 tablespoon of the sugar, some black pepper, and ½ tablespoon of the cornstarch. Set the mixture aside.

Put the noodles or vermicelli into 3 quarts of boiling water. Start testing the noodles after three minutes and cook them until they are al dente. (If you are using vermicelli, start testing them after five minutes.) Drain the pasta in a colander and rinse it under very hot water. Drain the pasta again and transfer it to a serving platter. Cover the platter with aluminum foil to keep the pasta warm.

Heat 2 teaspoons of the oil in a large, nonstick skillet or well-seasoned wok over high heat. Add the onion slices and stir-fry them for one minute. Add the carrot and broccoli, and stir-fry them for one minute. Add the red-pepper strips to the ingredients in the pan and stir-fry the mixture for two minutes more. Mound the vegetables on top of the pasta, cover the platter with the foil once more, and keep it warm.

Heat the remaining 2 teaspoons of oil in the skillet over high heat. Add the ginger and garlic, and stir-fry them until the ginger is light brown—about two min-utes. Add the beef along with its marinade, and stir-fry it until no traces of pink remain—one to two minutes. Spoon the beef mixture onto the center of the vege-tables and keep the platter warm.

Pour the stock into the skillet or wok, and bring it to a boil. While the stock is heating, mix the remaining cornstarch with 2 tablespoons of water in a small bowl. Stir into the stock the cornstarch mixture, the chili sauce or hot-red-pepper-flake mixture, the remaining tablespoon of sugar, the lemon juice, and the hoisin sauce or soy sauce. Lower the heat and simmer the mixture until it thickens—about one minute. Pour the sauce over the beef and serve it immediately.

# Orange-Fried Beef

Serves 6
Working (and total) time: about 45 minutes

Calories **270**
Protein **24g.**
Cholesterol **63mg.**
Total fat **10g.**
Saturated fat **3g.**
Sodium **140mg.**

| |
|---|
| 1½ lb. boneless sirloin steak, trimmed of fat and sliced into very thin strips |
| 2 oranges |
| 1 tbsp. grated lemon zest |
| 3 tbsp. cornstarch |
| 2 tbsp. sugar |
| 2 tbsp. safflower oil |
| 2 tsp. julienned fresh ginger |
| ¼ tsp. salt |
| ⅛ tsp. cayenne pepper |
| ¼ cup rice vinegar or distilled white vinegar |
| 1 lb. snow peas, stems and strings removed |

Carefully pare the zest from the oranges with a sharp knife, leaving the white pith behind. Slice the zest into fine julienne—you should have about ½ cup—and reserve it.

Squeeze the juice from the oranges and pour it into a small, nonreactive saucepan. Boil the juice over me-dium heat until only 3 tablespoons remain; set it aside.

Put the beef into a large bowl, and sprinkle it with the lemon zest, cornstarch, and sugar. Mix well to coat the beef, and set the beef aside.

Heat 1 tablespoon of the safflower oil in a large, nonstick skillet or a well-seasoned wok over high heat. Add the orange zest and the ginger to the skillet or wok, and cook them, stirring constantly, for one minute. Remove the zest and ginger with a slotted spoon, and set the mixture aside.

Add one-third of the beef to the hot skillet or wok, distributing it in a single layer. Brown the beef well—it should take three to four minutes to cook—stirring it frequently. With a slotted spoon, remove the cooked beef. Add ½ tablespoon of the oil to the skillet or wok and repeat the process with another third of the beef. Remove the second batch. Heat the remaining ½ ta-blespoon of oil and cook the rest of the meat.

Once the third batch is well browned, return the already-cooked beef and the zest and ginger mixture to the skillet or wok. Sprinkle the meat with the salt and the cayenne pepper, then pour in the vinegar and the reduced orange juice. Cook the meat rapidly, stir-ring often, until all the liquid has evaporated—ap-proximately two minutes.

While the beef is cooking, pour enough water into a saucepan to cover the bottom by 1 inch. Set a veg-etable steamer in the water, bring the water to a boil, and add the snow peas. Cover the pan tightly and steam the peas for two minutes.

Transfer the peas to a warmed serving platter and mound the beef on top. Serve immediately.

SUGGESTED ACCOMPANIMENT: *steamed rice.*

## Sautéed Beef Tossed with Red Cabbage and Apples

Serves 8
Working time: about 30 minutes
Total time: about 45 minutes

Calories **220**
Protein **19g.**
Cholesterol **50mg.**
Total fat **7g.**
Saturated fat **2g.**
Sodium **145mg.**

| |
| --- |
| 1¾ lb. sirloin steak, trimmed of fat and cut into thin strips about 1½ inches long |
| ¼ cup chopped shallots |
| ¼ tsp. salt |
| 1 cup unsalted brown stock or unsalted chicken stock (recipes, page 138) |
| 2 cups red wine |
| 2 tsp. caraway seeds |
| 1 small red cabbage (about 2½ lb.), cored, quartered, and sliced |
| 2 tart green apples, cored, quartered, and cut into strips 2 inches long and ¼ inch wide |
| 1 tbsp. honey |
| ¼ cup fresh lemon juice |
| freshly ground black pepper |
| 1½ tbsp. safflower oil |
| 2 scallions, trimmed and sliced |

Combine the shallots, salt, stock, wine, and 1 teaspoon of the caraway seeds in a nonreactive saucepan over medium heat. Simmer the liquid until it is reduced to ½ cup—about 40 minutes.

Meanwhile, place the cabbage in a bowl with the apples and the remaining teaspoon of caraway seeds. Mix the honey and lemon juice, and pour it over the cabbage mixture. Toss the mixture well and set it aside.

Place the meat in a bowl and sprinkle it with the pepper. Pour the reduced liquid over the meat and stir the mixture well.

Heat 1 tablespoon of the oil in a large, heavy-bottomed skillet set over high heat. Add the beef and scallions and sauté them, stirring, until the meat is browned—about one and a half minutes. Transfer the mixture to a bowl.

Heat the remaining ½ tablespoon of safflower oil in the skillet over medium-high heat. Add the cabbage and apple mixture and cook it, stirring frequently, until the cabbage has wilted slightly—three to four minutes. Return the beef to the skillet, toss the mixture well, and serve it at once.

SUGGESTED ACCOMPANIMENT: *broad egg noodles.*

## Stir-Fried Ginger Beef with Watercress

Serves 4
Working time: about 20 minutes
Total time: about 1 hour and 10 minutes

Calories **195**
Protein **21g.**
Cholesterol **54mg.**
Total fat **7g.**
Saturated fat **2g.**
Sodium **440mg.**

| |
| --- |
| 1 lb. top round steak, trimmed of fat and sliced into thin strips 3 inches long |
| ½ tbsp. peanut oil |
| 1 bunch watercress, trimmed, washed, and dried |

**Ginger marinade**

| |
| --- |
| 2-inch piece fresh ginger, peeled and finely chopped |
| 1 tbsp. chili paste, or 1 tsp. hot red-pepper flakes |
| ¼ cup dry sherry |
| ¼ cup unsalted chicken stock (recipe, page 138) |
| 1 tsp. cornstarch |
| 1 tsp. sugar |

**Cucumber salad**

| |
| --- |
| 2 cucumbers, seeded and cut into thick strips |
| ¼ tsp. salt |
| ¼ cup rice vinegar or distilled white vinegar |
| 1 tsp. dark sesame oil |

Combine all of the marinade ingredients in a bowl. Add the beef and toss it well; cover the bowl and marinate the meat for one hour at room temperature.

To make the salad, combine the cucumbers, salt, vinegar, and sesame oil in a bowl. Refrigerate the salad until serving time.

When the marinating time is up, drain the beef, reserving the marinade. Heat the oil in a large, nonstick skillet or a well-seasoned wok over high heat. Add the beef and stir-fry it until it is well browned—about two minutes. Add the reserved marinade; stir constantly until the sauce thickens—about one minute. Add the watercress and toss the mixture quickly. Serve the stir-fried beef and watercress immediately, accompanied by the chilled cucumber salad.

SUGGESTED ACCOMPANIMENT: *rice with sweet red peppers.*

# Viennese-Style Veal Cutlets

Serves 4
Working (and total) time: about 45 minutes

Calories **255**
Protein **22g.**
Cholesterol **90mg.**
Total fat **12g.**
Saturated fat **2g.**
Sodium **210mg.**

| |
| --- |
| *4 veal cutlets (about 3 oz. each), trimmed of fat and flattened (page 32, Step 1)* |
| *3 tbsp. rolled oats* |
| *¼ cup unbleached all-purpose flour* |
| *¼ tsp. salt* |
| *freshly ground black pepper* |
| *1 egg white* |
| *2 tbsp. safflower oil* |
| *lemon wedges for garnish* |

Grind the rolled oats to fine crumbs in a blender or food processor. Put the flour, salt, and pepper on a large plate or sheet of wax paper, mix them together, and spread out evenly. Lightly beat the egg white with 1 tablespoon of water in a small bowl. Spread out the rolled oats on another plate or sheet of wax paper.

Dip one cutlet in the seasoned flour to coat both sides, and shake off the excess flour. Place the cutlet on a flat surface and lightly brush the egg white over one side. Turn the cutlet over, and place it on the plate of rolled oats, egg side down. Press down gently. Brush the top side of the cutlet with egg white, turn it over, and press it gently into the oats. Cover any still-exposed areas of cutlet with oats so that it is evenly coated, pressing the oats on gently with your fingertips. Shake off the excess oats. Coat the remaining cutlets in the same way.

Heat 1 tablespoon of the oil in a heavy-bottomed, nonstick skillet over medium heat. Add two of the cutlets and cook for five to seven minutes in all, turning to brown evenly. When cooked, transfer the cutlets to a warm platter. Cook the remaining cutlets in the same way. Garnish with the lemon wedges and serve.

SUGGESTED ACCOMPANIMENT: *fresh spinach.*

# Veal, Prosciutto, and Sage Sauté

Serves 4
Working (and total) time: about 15 minutes

Calories **175**
Protein **23g.**
Cholesterol **95mg.**
Total fat **7g.**
Saturated fat **2g.**
Sodium **350mg.**

14 oz. veal rump, trimmed of fat, cut
into strips ¼ inch wide
and 1½ inches long

1 tbsp. virgin olive oil

1½ oz. thinly sliced prosciutto, trimmed
of excess fat, cut into
strips ¼ inch wide and 1½
inches long

¼ tsp. salt

freshly ground black pepper

3 tbsp. coarsely chopped fresh sage,
or 2 tsp. dried sage

¼ cup Marsala

Heat the olive oil in a large, nonstick skillet over high heat. Add the strips of veal and sauté it for about one and a half minutes, stirring to cook and brown them evenly. If the veal gives up a lot of liquid, cook until it has evaporated.

Add the strips of prosciutto, the salt, and some pepper, and cook the meat, stirring and tossing, for one minute. Add the sage and Marsala, toss for 30 seconds more, and serve immediately.

SUGGESTED ACCOMPANIMENTS: *creamed potato and celeriac sprinkled with chives; watercress and orange salad.*

# Veal Cutlets with Lemon and Asparagus

Serves 4
Working (and total) time: about 30 minutes

Calories **180**
Protein **23g.**
Cholesterol **90mg.**
Total fat **10g.**
Saturated fat **3g.**
Sodium **380mg.**

| |
| --- |
| 4 veal cutlets (about 3 oz. each), trimmed of fat and flattened (page 32, Step 1) |
| 4 large asparagus spears |
| 1 tbsp. virgin olive oil |
| 1 garlic clove, quartered |
| ½ lemon, juice only |
| ½ tbsp. chopped fresh rosemary, or ½ tsp. dried rosemary, crumbled |
| ¼ tsp. salt |
| freshly ground black pepper |
| 1½ tbsp. freshly grated Parmesan cheese |

Cook the asparagus in a small, shallow pan of boiling water for two to three minutes, or until it is just tender but still firm. Drain the asparagus and refresh it under cold running water to prevent further cooking. Drain again, cut the asparagus spears in half lengthwise, and set them aside while you cook the meat.

Preheat the broiler for 10 minutes.

Slice each cutlet crosswise into three pieces. Heat the olive oil with the quartered garlic clove in a large, nonstick skillet over high heat. Add half of the veal and cook for about one and a half minutes in all, or until the pieces are golden brown on both sides. Transfer the veal to a gratin dish, and cook the remaining veal in the same way. Arrange the pieces of veal in the bottom of the dish, overlapping them slightly. Sprinkle them with the lemon juice, rosemary, salt, and some black pepper. Discard the garlic.

Arrange the halved asparagus spears attractively on top of the veal pieces. Sprinkle the Parmesan cheese over the veal and asparagus. Broil for three to four minutes, or until the veal and asparagus are piping hot and the topping is golden brown. Serve immediately.

SUGGESTED ACCOMPANIMENT: *mushroom risotto.*

## Sichuan Stir-Fried Veal and Crunchy Vegetables

Serves 4
Working time: about 40 minutes
Total time: about 2 hours and 40 minutes
(includes marinating)

Calories **300**
Protein **30g.**
Cholesterol **110mg.**
Total fat **14g.**
Saturated fat **3g.**
Sodium **215mg.**

| |
|---|
| 1 lb. veal cutlets, trimmed of fat, flattened (page 32, Step 1), and cut diagonally into strips 1½ inches long by ¼ inch wide |
| ¼ cup low-sodium soy sauce |
| ¼ cup sake or dry sherry |
| 2 dried red chili peppers, finely chopped (cautionary note, page 8) |
| 2 tbsp. safflower oil |
| 6 scallions, sliced diagonally |
| 1-inch piece fresh ginger, cut into very fine julienne |
| 1 to 2 garlic cloves, crushed |
| ¼ lb. whole baby corn (fresh or frozen) |
| ½ lb. carrots (2 to 3 medium), julienned |
| ¼ lb. cauliflower florets (about 1 cup) |
| ¼ lb. green beans, ends removed |
| ⅔ cup unsalted chicken stock or unsalted veal stock (recipes, page 138) |
| 1 tbsp. tomato paste |
| 1½ tbsp. cornstarch, mixed with 1 tbsp. cold water |
| freshly ground black pepper |
| 1 tbsp. sesame oil |

In a bowl, combine the strips of veal, 2 tablespoons each of the soy sauce and sake or dry sherry, and the chilies. Cover the veal and let it marinate for two hours, turning it occasionally.

Heat a wok or a large, deep, heavy-bottomed skillet over medium-high heat, and pour in the safflower oil. Add the scallions, ginger, and garlic, and stir-fry for 30 seconds to flavor the oil. Add the veal and its marinade, and stir-fry, tossing frequently, until all the strips have changed color—about three minutes. Remove the veal and flavorings with a slotted spoon, and set them aside on a plate; do not discard the oil.

Add the baby corn to the pan and stir-fry, tossing constantly, for one minute, then add the carrots, cauliflower, and beans, and stir-fry for two minutes more. Return the veal and flavorings to the pan, and stir-fry to combine the veal strips with the vegetables. Push the contents to the sides and pour the stock into the center of the pan. Stir in the tomato paste, the remaining soy sauce and sake or sherry, the cornstarch mixture, and some pepper. Bring to a boil and boil until the liquid thickens—one to two minutes. Redistribute the veal and vegetables in the sauce, and stir to coat all the ingredients evenly.

Serve the veal and vegetables with the sesame oil sprinkled over the top.

SUGGESTED ACCOMPANIMENT: *Chinese egg noodles.*

## Medallions of Veal with Rosemary and Red Wine

Serves 6
Working time: about 15 minutes
Total time: about 1 hour and 15 minutes
(includes marinating)

Calories **200**
Protein **21g.**
Cholesterol **95mg.**
Total fat **12g.**
Saturated fat **3g.**
Sodium **215mg.**

| |
|---|
| 6 medallions of veal (about 4 oz. each), trimmed of fat |
| 12 or more sprigs rosemary |
| 2 tbsp. virgin olive oil |
| 1 garlic clove, crushed |
| 1 lemon, finely grated zest only |

| |
|---|
| 1 tbsp. chopped fresh parsley |
| 1 tbsp. unsalted butter |
| 1 cup red wine |
| ⅔ cup unsalted veal stock or unsalted chicken stock (recipes, page 138) |
| ¼ tsp. salt |
| freshly ground black pepper |

Spear each medallion of veal with two or three small rosemary sprigs. Blend 1½ tablespoons of the oil with the garlic, lemon zest, and parsley in a shallow dish. Add the medallions to this marinade and turn them carefully until they are well coated. Cover and marinate at room temperature for at least one hour.

Heat the remaining oil with the butter in a nonstick skillet. Add the medallions and cook for two to three minutes on each side, until they are well browned but still slightly pink inside. Transfer the veal to a plate lined with paper towels. Cover and keep hot.

Pour off all the excess fat from the skillet, and stir in the wine and stock. Bring to a boil, stirring, then boil gently until the liquid is reduced by half. Season with the salt and some pepper.

Arrange the medallions on a hot serving plate, strain the sauce over them and, if desired, garnish with more rosemary sprigs. Serve immediately.

SUGGESTED ACCOMPANIMENT: *green beans or asparagus.*

# Veal Cutlets with Gorgonzola and Fennel

Serves 4
Working (and total) time: about 40 minutes

Calories **240**
Protein **27g.**
Cholesterol **105mg.**
Total fat **12g.**
Saturated fat **2g.**
Sodium **380mg.**

| |
|---|
| *one 1-lb. piece loin of veal, trimmed of fat, cut diagonally into ¼-inch-thick slices and slightly flattened (page 32, Step 1)* |
| *1 tbsp. virgin olive oil* |
| *2 tbsp. anise-flavored liqueur or unsalted veal stock or unsalted chicken stock (recipes, page 138)* |
| *1 large fennel bulb, cut into slices, feathery tops reserved* |
| *3 oz. Gorgonzola cheese, mashed* |
| *2 tbsp. skim milk* |
| *2 tsp. chopped fresh sage, or ½ tsp. dried sage* |
| *2 tsp. chopped fresh thyme, or ½ tsp. dried thyme leaves* |
| *⅛ tsp. salt* |
| *freshly ground black pepper* |

Preheat the oven to 275° F. Heat the oil in a nonstick skillet over medium-high heat, add as many pieces of veal as the pan will comfortably hold, and cook them for three to five minutes until they are just tender, turning once and pressing the pieces of veal firmly with a spatula to keep them as flat as possible. Transfer the veal to a platter, cover, and keep it hot in the oven. Cook the remainder of the veal in the same way.

Add the anise-flavored liqueur or stock to the cooking juices in the pan, increase the heat, and stir briskly to deglaze. Add the fennel and toss over high heat for two to three minutes, then remove it with a slotted spoon and keep it hot with the veal.

Lower the heat, add the Gorgonzola and milk, and cook gently, stirring, until the cheese has melted and formed a sauce with the cooking juices and milk. Add the chopped sage, thyme, salt, and some pepper, and remove the pan from the heat.

To assemble the dish, arrange the meat and fennel on individual plates. Spoon the sauce over the meat and garnish with the reserved fennel tops. Serve the dish immediately.

EDITOR'S NOTE: *Adding anise-flavored liqueur to the cooking juices heightens the flavor of the fennel.*

*3* *Flattened veal cutlets await a fruit stuffing and a gentle simmering in red grape juice (recipe, page 100).*

# Moist and Gentle Cooking

Braising, poaching, and stewing are all moist methods of cooking that involve simmering meat in the liquid and steam of an enclosed vessel. They differ from each other only in that braising employs relatively little liquid compared with poaching, and often, the meat to be braised is browned initially to produce rich residues that contribute flavor to the finished dish. Stewing generally implies the braising of meat that has been cut into small pieces.

The appeal of moist methods lies in a culinary alchemy whereby the flavor of the meat, and of any supporting vegetables and herbs, is drawn into the surrounding liquid. The most commonly used liquids are stock, wine, and water. But there are no hard-and-fast rules. Beer, for example, might be used *(page 84)*, and tomatoes, puréed or chopped, feature often—as in the recipes on pages 87, 90, 97, and 101.

Traditionally, cooks have employed the moist methods for the tougher cuts of beef and veal, since these cuts have most to gain from the tenderizing process of prolonged moist cooking. But the health-conscious cook must question some of the old ways, since many of the tougher cuts are excessively fatty. In breast of veal and beef flank, for example, the layers of muscle are interlarded with fat, and the marrow in the center of a slice of veal shin is very high in fat. In place of such cuts, the recipes here make much use of beef and veal round and beef sirloin.

These less fatty cuts, having also less gristle, do not necessarily need—or profit from—extensive simmering. In the case of fruit-stuffed veal olives *(page 100)*, for example, cutlets are simmered for just 20 minutes in red grape juice, after a brief preliminary browning. In Japanese simmered beef *(page 99)*, slices of beef tenderloin are cooked at the table in a highly seasoned broth for a mere five minutes.

As well as avoiding fatty cuts, this chapter also looks to supporting ingredients to play a part in keeping the calorie count low. Gone is the excess of flour, egg yolks, and cream that once played a part in the thickening of cooking liquids. Many of the new sauces are thickened by reduction. In the case of the blanquette of veal *(page 104)*, the conventional thickening of several egg yolks and heavy cream is replaced with a single egg yolk, low-fat milk, and cornstarch. Accompanied by mushrooms and onions and seasoned with lemon juice, the result is a light and refreshing reinterpretation of the culinary classic.

# Sauerbraten

IN THIS LEAN VERSION OF A POPULAR GERMAN DISH, TOP ROUND IS MARINATED IN WINE VINEGAR, SUGAR, AND SPICES FOR THREE DAYS TO PRODUCE MOIST, TENDER BEEF.

Serves 6
Working time: about 45 minutes
Total time: about 3 days (includes marinating)

Calories **340**
Protein **40g.**
Cholesterol **75mg.**
Total fat **6g.**
Saturated fat **3g.**
Sodium **200mg.**

| |
|---|
| 2 lb. beef top round, trimmed of fat, rolled and tied |
| 10 whole cloves |
| 1 cup red wine |
| ½ cup red wine vinegar |
| 1 onion, grated |
| 2 tsp. light brown sugar |
| 1 tsp. dry mustard |
| 6 black peppercorns |
| 2 bay leaves |
| ½ tsp. ground allspice |
| 1 tbsp. virgin olive oil |
| ⅔ cup brown stock (recipe, page 138) |
| 3 lb. mixed root vegetables (turnip, parsnip, rutabaga, carrot, potato), peeled and left whole or cut into large chunks |
| 3 tbsp. raisins |
| 2 tsp. arrowroot |
| freshly ground black pepper |
| ⅛ tsp. salt |
| 2 tbsp. finely chopped fresh parsley |

Stud the beef with the cloves and place it in a non-reactive dish. In a nonreactive saucepan, heat the red wine, wine vinegar, onion, sugar, mustard, peppercorns, bay leaves, and allspice. Pour the mixture over the beef and let it cool. When the beef has cooled completely, cover the dish and marinate the beef in the refrigerator for three days, turning it occasionally.

Thirty minutes before cooking, remove the beef from the marinade, pat it dry with paper towels, and let it stand at room temperature. Reserve the marinade. Preheat the oven to 300° F.

Heat the oil in a flameproof casserole over high heat, add the beef, and brown it on all sides, turning it constantly—about five minutes. Strain the reserved marinade over the beef, pour in the stock, and bring to a boil. Cover the beef and cook it in the oven for one and a quarter hours, turning and basting it frequently. Meanwhile, put the root vegetables into a large saucepan, cover them with cold water, and bring to a boil. Drain the vegetables immediately and set them aside.

Remove the casserole from the oven and arrange the vegetables around the meat as shown on the left. Cover the casserole again and return it to the oven for one hour more, or until the beef and vegetables are tender and cooked through.

Transfer the beef to a warmed serving dish. Remove the vegetables from the cooking liquid with a slotted spoon and arrange them around the beef. Set the dish aside and keep it hot. Transfer the casserole to the top of the stove and add the raisins. Mix the arrowroot to a smooth paste with 1 tablespoon of cold water and stir it into the cooking liquid. Bring the liquid to a boil, stirring, then simmer it until it has thickened—two to three minutes. Add some pepper and the salt. Serve the meat sliced, with a little of the gravy poured over it. Sprinkle the vegetables with the parsley and pass the remaining gravy separately.

SUGGESTED ACCOMPANIMENT: *mashed potatoes.*

# Beef Braised in Beer

Serves 8
Working time: about 30 minutes
Total time: about 3 hours

Calories **290**
Protein **31g.**
Cholesterol **85mg.**
Total fat **8g.**
Saturated fat **3g.**
Sodium **240mg.**

| |
|---|
| one 2½-lb. arm pot roast, trimmed of fat |
| ½ tsp. safflower oil |
| 8 large onions (about 4 lb.), sliced |
| 2 cups unsalted brown stock or unsalted chicken stock (recipes, page 138) |
| 2 tbsp. unbleached all-purpose flour |
| 12 oz. dark beer |
| 4 garlic cloves, chopped |
| 2 tbsp. julienned fresh ginger |
| 1 bay leaf |
| 4 sprigs fresh thyme, or 1 tsp. dried thyme leaves |
| 1 strip of lemon zest |
| 2 tbsp. dark molasses |
| ½ tsp. salt |
| freshly ground black pepper |

Preheat the oven to 325° F. Heat the oil in a large, nonstick skillet over high heat. Add the pot roast and sear it until it is well browned on both sides—about five minutes in all. Transfer the roast to an ovenproof casserole or Dutch oven.

Reduce the heat under the skillet to medium. Add the onions to the skillet and cook them, stirring frequently, until they begin to soften—about 10 minutes. Deglaze the pan with two tablespoons of the stock. Continue cooking the onions, adding another two tablespoons of stock whenever the liquid in the skillet has evaporated, until the onions are very soft and their juices have caramelized—15 to 20 minutes more. Sprinkle the flour over the onions; cook the mixture, stirring constantly, for one minute.

Pour 1 cup of the remaining stock into the skillet and stir well to incorporate the flour. Increase the heat to medium high and boil the mixture until it is quite thick—three to four minutes. Pour in the rest of the stock and the beer. Bring the liquid to a simmer, then transfer the contents of the skillet to the casserole or Dutch oven. Add the garlic, ginger, bay leaf, thyme, lemon zest, molasses, salt, and some pepper. Cover the casserole and braise the roast in the oven until it is very tender—about two hours.

Transfer the roast to a cutting board, slice it, and arrange the slices on a serving platter. Remove the bay leaf, the thyme sprigs if you used them, and the lemon zest from the sauce, and pour it over the meat.

SUGGESTED ACCOMPANIMENTS: *noodles tossed with fresh parsley; steamed parsnips.*

# Lemon-Cardamom Braised Beef

Serves 8
Working time: about 1 hour
Total time: about 3 hours

Calories **240**
Protein **29g.**
Cholesterol **78mg.**
Total fat **8g.**
Saturated fat **3g.**
Sodium **290mg.**

| |
| --- |
| one 3-lb. tip roast, trimmed of fat |
| 2 tsp. safflower oil |
| 2 onions, cut into eighths |
| 2 celery stalks, coarsely chopped |
| 2 garlic cloves, chopped |
| 3 cups unsalted brown stock or unsalted chicken stock (recipes, page 138) |
| ½ cup dry white wine |
| zest of 1 lemon, cut into strips |
| ½ tsp. ground cardamom or ground ginger |
| ½ tsp. salt |
| 2½ tbsp. fresh lemon juice |
| 1 tbsp. Dijon mustard |
| freshly ground black pepper |
| 1 lb. carrots |
| 1 lb. zucchini, halved lengthwise, the halves sliced on the diagonal into ½-inch-wide pieces |

Heat the oil in a Dutch oven or a large, deep, nonstick skillet over high heat. Sear the beef until it is browned on all sides—10 to 15 minutes. Tuck the onions, celery, and garlic around the beef, and add the stock, wine, lemon zest, ¼ teaspoon of the cardamom or ginger, and ¼ teaspoon of the salt. Bring the liquid to a boil, then lower the heat to maintain a slow simmer. Cover the skillet, leaving the lid slightly ajar, and braise the beef for one hour. Turn the beef over and continue cooking it until it is tender—one hour and 30 minutes to two hours. Transfer the beef to a cutting board and cover it loosely with aluminum foil.

Strain the cooking liquid through a fine sieve into a nonreactive saucepan. Whisk in 1½ tablespoons of the lemon juice, the mustard, a generous grinding of pepper, the remaining ¼ teaspoon of cardamom or ginger, and the remaining ¼ teaspoon of salt. Cook the sauce over medium heat until it is reduced to 1¼ cups.

While the sauce is reducing, peel the carrots and cut them with a roll cut: Using a chef's knife, slice off the tip of a carrot on the diagonal. Roll the carrot a half-turn and slice off another piece—it will have nonparallel ends. Continue rolling and slicing until you reach the stem end. Repeat the procedure to prepare the remaining carrots.

Pour enough water into a saucepan to fill it 1 inch ▶

deep. Set a vegetable steamer in the pan and bring the water to a boil. Add the carrots and cover the pan tightly. Steam the carrots until they begin to soften—five to seven minutes. Transfer them to a large, non-reactive skillet set over medium-high heat. Add the zucchini, the remaining 1 tablespoon of lemon juice, ½ cup of the sauce, and a liberal grinding of pepper. Cook the vegetables, stirring frequently, until almost all of the liquid has evaporated and the vegetables are glazed—7 to 10 minutes.

Cut the beef into thin slices and arrange them on a warmed serving platter along with the vegetables. Briefly reheat the remaining sauce and pour it over the beef. Serve immediately.

SUGGESTED ACCOMPANIMENT: *whole-grain muffins.*

## Beef Braised with Fennel

Serves 4
Working time: about 15 minutes
Total time: about 1 hour and 15 minutes

Calories **245**
Protein **27g.**
Cholesterol **76mg.**
Total fat **10g.**
Saturated fat **3g.**
Sodium **250mg.**

| |
|---|
| one 1¼-lb. boneless sirloin steak, trimmed of fat and cut into 4 pieces |
| ¼ tsp. salt |
| freshly ground black pepper |
| 1 tbsp. safflower oil |
| 1 large fennel bulb, thinly sliced |
| 1 cup unsalted brown stock or unsalted chicken stock (recipes, page 138) |
| ¼ cup dry white wine |
| 1 large carrot, peeled and grated |
| 1 tbsp. cornstarch, mixed with 2 tablespoons of water |

With a meat mallet or the flat of a heavy knife, pound the steak pieces to a thickness of ½ inch. Season the meat with the salt and some pepper. Heat 1 teaspoon of the oil in a large, nonstick skillet over medium-high heat and sear the meat on both sides. Transfer the meat to a plate and set it aside.

Heat the remaining 2 teaspoons of oil in the skillet and add the fennel. Cook the fennel, stirring occasionally, until it begins to brown—10 to 12 minutes. Return the meat to the skillet. Pour in the stock and white wine and, if necessary, enough water to raise the liquid level two-thirds up the side of the meat. Bring the liquid to a simmer, cover the skillet, and braise the meat for 25 minutes. Turn the pieces and continue cooking them for 20 minutes.

Stir the carrot into the skillet and cook it for 10 minutes. Whisk the cornstarch mixture into the simmering liquid; stir constantly until the sauce thickens slightly. Serve the beef and fennel immediately.

SUGGESTED ACCOMPANIMENT: *lettuce and tomato salad.*

# Roulades in Tomato Sauce

Serves 8
Working time: about 1 hour and 30 minutes
Total time: about 4 hours

Calories **235**
Protein **25g.**
Cholesterol **57mg.**
Total fat **8g.**
Saturated fat **3g.**
Sodium **165mg.**

| |
|---|
| one 2-lb. beef top round roast, trimmed of fat and cut on the diagonal into 16 scaloppine |
| 1 tsp. safflower oil |
| 3 onions, finely chopped |
| 4 garlic cloves, finely chopped |
| 2 carrots, finely chopped |
| 56 oz. canned unsalted whole tomatoes, with their juice |
| 2 bay leaves |
| 3 tbsp. chopped fresh parsley |
| 2 tbsp. chopped fresh oregano, or 2 tsp. dried oregano |
| ½ cup dry breadcrumbs |
| ¼ cup freshly grated Parmesan cheese |
| 2 tbsp. finely chopped prosciutto or boiled ham |
| ¼ cup dry white wine |

Mix the oil, onions, garlic, and carrots in a large, heavy-bottomed saucepan. Cover the pan and cook the mixture over low heat until the onions are translucent—about 15 minutes.

Purée the tomatoes in a food processor or a blender. Add the tomato purée and bay leaves to the onion and carrot mixture. Increase the heat to medium and simmer the vegetables, uncovered, until they become a thick sauce—about two hours.

While the sauce is simmering, make the roulades. In a bowl, combine the parsley, oregano, breadcrumbs, cheese, prosciutto or ham, and wine. Spread the scaloppine flat on the work surface and spread some of the stuffing mixture on each one. Roll up each slice and tie it with two short pieces of string to secure it.

Add the roulades to the thickened sauce and simmer them until the meat is tender—about one hour. Lift the roulades from the sauce and remove the string. Transfer the roulades to a serving platter or individual plates, spoon the sauce over them, and serve them at once.

SUGGESTED ACCOMPANIMENT: *fettuccine.*

## Cabbage Rolls with Beef and Sage

Serves 6
Working time: about 45 minutes
Total time: about 2 hours and 15 minutes

Calories **305**
Protein **27g.**
Cholesterol **60mg.**
Total fat **9g.**
Saturated fat **3g.**
Sodium **250mg.**

| |
|---|
| one 1½-lb. top round steak, trimmed of fat and cut on the diagonal into 12 thin slices |
| 1 large green cabbage (about 4 lb.) |
| 1 tbsp. safflower oil |
| 2 cups chopped onion |
| 1 tbsp. chopped fresh sage, or 1 tsp. dried sage |
| 4 garlic cloves, finely chopped |
| 3 slices white bread, crumbled |
| ½ cup stemmed parsley sprigs |
| 28 oz. canned unsalted whole tomatoes, crushed in their juice |
| 3 carrots, thinly sliced |
| 3 tbsp. cider vinegar |
| 1½ tbsp. sugar |
| ¼ tsp. salt |
| freshly ground black pepper |

Carefully remove 12 large outer leaves from the cabbage. Cut a small, V-shaped wedge from each leaf to remove the tough core. Cook the leaves in a large pot of boiling water until they are translucent and limp—about 10 minutes. Drain the leaves in a colander.

Finely slice enough of the remaining cabbage to yield 5 cups. Save the rest for use in another recipe.

To prepare the filling, heat the oil in a large, heavy-bottomed, nonstick skillet over medium heat. Add the sliced cabbage, 1½ cups of the onion, 2 teaspoons of the fresh sage or ½ teaspoon of the dried sage, and half of the garlic. Cook the mixture, stirring occasionally, until the onion is translucent and the cabbage is soft—about 10 minutes. Transfer the mixture to a bowl, add the bread and parsley, and toss well. Set the filling aside.

Meanwhile, put the tomatoes and their juice, the remaining garlic, the carrots, and ¾ cup of water into a very large, nonreactive skillet. Cook the mixture, stirring occasionally, over low heat for 15 minutes. Add the remaining ½ cup of onion, the remaining sage, the vinegar, the sugar, the salt, and some pepper. Allow the sauce to simmer slowly while you prepare the rolls.

With a meat mallet or the flat of a heavy knife, pound the beef slices between two pieces of heavy-duty plastic wrap to a thickness of ⅛ inch. Sprinkle the slices with some pepper.

Set a cabbage leaf on the work surface with the stem end toward you. Lay a beef slice on top of the leaf, then mound 2 heaping tablespoons of the filling on the beef. Roll up the leaf starting at the stem end; fold in the sides over the filling as you go. Repeat the process with the remaining leaves, meat, and filling.

Place the cabbage rolls, seam side down, in the simmering sauce. Cook the rolls, with the skillet lid slightly ajar, over low to medium-low heat for one hour and 15 minutes. Carefully transfer the rolls to a platter. Spoon the sauce over them and serve immediately.

SUGGESTED ACCOMPANIMENT: *barley and mushroom pilaf.*

# Braised Cinnamon Beef Roll

Serves 4
Working time: about 25 minutes
Total time: about 2 hours

Calories **250**
Protein **28g.**
Cholesterol **72mg.**
Total fat **11g.**
Saturated fat **3g.**
Sodium **215mg.**

| |
|---|
| one 1¼-lb. top round, rump, or tip roast, trimmed of fat and cut into 4 slices |
| 1 tbsp. ground cinnamon |
| ¼ tsp. salt |
| freshly ground black pepper |
| 1 tbsp. safflower oil |
| 1 large onion, thinly sliced |
| 1 garlic clove, finely chopped |
| 2 cinnamon sticks |
| ½ cup dry white wine |
| 1 cup unsalted brown stock or unsalted chicken stock (recipes, page 138) |
| 1 tbsp. cornstarch, mixed with 1 tbsp. of the stock |

Place the beef slices between two sheets of heavy-duty plastic wrap or wax paper, and pound them with a meat mallet or the flat of a heavy knife to a thickness of ⅛ inch. Sprinkle the meat with the ground cinnamon, the salt, and some pepper. Overlap the edges of two slices, spiced side up; cover the seam thus formed with plastic wrap or wax paper and lightly pound the overlapping edges to join the slices. Join the remaining two slices by the same procedure.

Place one of the joined pieces on top of the other, again spiced side up, then roll them up tightly, starting with one of the longer edges. To hold the roll together, tie it with butcher's twine (*technique, page 25*).

Heat 1 teaspoon of the oil in a heavy-bottomed, nonreactive skillet over medium-high heat and sear the beef on all sides. Remove the meat; add the remaining 2 teaspoons of oil and the onion to the skillet, and cook the onion over medium heat, stirring occasionally, until it is translucent—four to five minutes. Stir in the garlic, cinnamon sticks, wine, and stock. Return the beef to the skillet and, if necessary, pour in enough water to half submerge the roll. Bring the liquid to a simmer, cover the skillet tightly, and continue simmering the

roll until the meat feels tender when pierced with the tip of a sharp knife—one hour and 15 minutes to one hour and 30 minutes.

When the beef roll is cooked, transfer it to a plate. Increase the heat to medium high and bring the liquid in the skillet to a boil. Remove the cinnamon sticks and discard them. Whisk the cornstarch paste into the liquid, whisking continuously until the sauce thickens—about 30 seconds.

Remove the string, cut the meat into thin slices, and place the slices on a warm serving platter. Top them with some of the sauce, pouring the rest around the beef. Serve immediately.

SUGGESTED ACCOMPANIMENT: *brown rice tossed with scallions and raisins.*

brown it on both sides—one to two minutes per side—then pour in the stock and enough water to cover the meat. Add the tomato purée, garlic, salt, peppercorns, bay leaf, and thyme, and bring the liquid to a boil. Reduce the heat to low, cover the casserole, and simmer the beef until it feels very tender when pierced with a fork—two to three hours. Remove the pot roast from the casserole without discarding the cooking liquid; keep the roast warm.

Add the carrots, the celeriac or celery, the onions, and the parsnips or turnips to the cooking liquid. Simmer the vegetables until they are tender—approximately 20 minutes.

Cut the pot roast into neat slices and arrange them on a serving platter. Surround the meat with the vegetables. Spoon some of the cooking liquid over the pot roast, and pour the rest of it into a gravy boat to be passed separately.

## Braised Steak with Onions

Serves 6
Working time: about 30 minutes
Total time: about 2 hours and 30 minutes

Calories **175**
Protein **22g.**
Cholesterol **49mg.**
Total fat **5g.**
Saturated fat **2g.**
Sodium **195mg.**

| |
|---|
| one 1¾-lb. eye round roast, trimmed of fat and cut into 6 steaks |
| 2 tsp. safflower oil |
| 2 large onions, thinly sliced |
| 2 cups red wine |
| 2 carrots, cut into bâtonnets |
| 1 celery stalk, chopped |
| ¼ tsp. salt |
| freshly ground black pepper |
| 2 cups unsalted brown stock or unsalted chicken stock (recipes, page 138) |

Preheat the oven to 325° F.

Heat the oil in a large, ovenproof, nonreactive skillet over medium heat. Add the onions and cook them, stirring frequently, until they are translucent and their juices have caramelized—5 to 10 minutes. Pour ½ cup of the wine into the skillet, increase the heat, and boil the wine until nearly all of the liquid has evaporated. Pour in another ½ cup and reduce this also. Boil away the remaining wine in two batches, stirring constantly as the last ½ cup begins to evaporate.

Add the carrots, celery, salt, some pepper, and the stock to the skillet. Lay the steaks on top of the vegetables; cover the skillet and transfer it to the oven. Braise the steaks until they are tender—one and a half to two hours. Serve the steaks topped with the vegetables and braising juices.

SUGGESTED ACCOMPANIMENT: *potatoes and rutabagas mashed together and sprinkled with chopped parsley.*

## Pot Roast with Parsnips

Serves 10
Working time: about 20 minutes
Total time: about 2 hours and 30 minutes

Calories **290**
Protein **33g.**
Cholesterol **93mg.**
Total fat **10g.**
Saturated fat **3g.**
Sodium **215mg.**

| |
|---|
| one 3½-lb. arm pot roast, trimmed of fat |
| 1 tbsp. safflower oil |
| 1 cup unsalted brown stock or unsalted chicken stock (recipes, page 138) |
| 14 oz. canned unsalted tomatoes, puréed and strained |
| 2 garlic cloves, finely chopped |
| ½ tsp. salt |
| 10 crushed black peppercorns |
| 1 bay leaf |
| 1 tbsp. chopped fresh thyme, or 1 tsp. dried thyme leaves |
| 3 carrots, peeled and cut diagonally into ½-inch-thick ovals |
| ¾ lb. celeriac, peeled and cut into ½-inch cubes, or 3 celery stalks, cut into ½-inch pieces |
| 5 small onions, peeled and halved crosswise |
| 1 lb. parsnips, peeled and cut into ½-inch pieces, or 1 lb. turnips, peeled and cut into ½-inch pieces |

Heat the safflower oil in a large, heavy-bottomed casserole over medium-high heat. Add the pot roast and

# Steak Braised in Spicy Vinegar Sauce

Serves 4
Working time: about 15 minutes
Total time: about 4 hours and 15 minutes
(includes marinating)

Calories **235**
Protein **28g.**
Cholesterol **78mg.**
Total fat **11g.**
Saturated fat **3g.**
Sodium **245mg.**

| |
|---|
| one 1¼-lb. boneless sirloin steak, trimmed of fat and cut into 4 pieces |
| 1 garlic clove, finely chopped |
| 1 tbsp. chopped fresh oregano, or 1 tsp. dried oregano |
| hot red-pepper flakes |
| ¼ cup balsamic vinegar, or 3 tbsp. red wine vinegar mixed with 1 tsp. honey |
| 1 tbsp. safflower oil |
| ¼ tsp. salt |
| freshly ground black pepper |
| 14 oz. canned unsalted whole tomatoes, with their juice |
| 2 tbsp. freshly grated Parmesan cheese |
| parsley sprigs for garnish |

Put the pieces of meat into a shallow, nonreactive dish and add the garlic, oregano, a pinch of red pepper flakes, and the vinegar. Let the meat marinate for three hours in the refrigerator. Drain the meat and pat the pieces dry, reserving the marinade.

Heat the safflower oil in a large, heavy-bottomed, nonreactive skillet over medium-high heat. Sear the meat on both sides, then season it with the salt and some black pepper. Purée the tomatoes in a food processor or a blender, and add them and the reserved marinade to the skillet. Cover the skillet and simmer the meat in the sauce for 30 minutes. Turn the meat, replace the cover, and continue braising the pieces until they are tender—30 to 45 minutes.

Transfer the beef to a heated platter and spoon the sauce over it. Serve the dish topped with the grated cheese and garnished with parsley sprigs.

---

SUGGESTED ACCOMPANIMENTS: *pasta tossed with some of the spicy vinegar sauce; steamed zucchini.*

# Red-Cooked Beef

Serves 6
Working time: about 30 minutes
Total time: about 2 hours and 30 minutes

Calories **270**
Protein **38g.**
Cholesterol **75mg.**
Total fat **8g.**
Saturated fat **3g.**
Sodium **105mg.**

| |
|---|
| 2 lb. beef round, trimmed of fat and cut into ¾-inch strips |
| 4 Chinese dried mushrooms, soaked in hot water for 10 to 15 minutes |
| 3 tbsp. low-sodium soy sauce |
| 2 tbsp. dry sherry |
| 2 tbsp. light brown sugar |
| 1 tbsp. tomato paste |
| 1-inch piece fresh ginger, peeled and crushed |
| 2 garlic cloves, crushed |
| ½ tsp. five-spice powder |
| 1 cup unsalted brown stock (recipe, page 138) |
| 1 tbsp. safflower oil |
| 3 medium carrots, thinly sliced diagonally |

Drain the mushrooms and gently squeeze out any excess moisture. Trim and slice them. Place them in a bowl with the soy sauce, sherry, brown sugar, tomato paste, ginger, garlic, five-spice powder, and stock. Stir well and set aside.

Heat the oil in a heavy, flameproof casserole over high heat. Add one-third of the beef pieces and brown them on all sides, turning them constantly—about three minutes. With a slotted spoon, drain the meat, then transfer it to a plate lined with paper towels. Repeat with the remaining two batches of beef, draining each batch on fresh towels. Return all the beef to the casserole, add the mushroom and stock mixture, and bring it slowly to a boil. Lower the heat, cover, and simmer very gently for one and a half hours, turning the meat over frequently during this time and basting it with the cooking liquid.

Add the carrots and continue cooking for 30 minutes more, or until the beef is tender; the carrots should be cooked but still firm. Serve hot.

SUGGESTED ACCOMPANIMENT: *stir-fried snow peas and bean sprouts.*

# Beef Daube Provençale

THIS LOW-FAT VERSION OF A FRENCH DAUBE USES GRAPE JUICE
IN THE MARINADE AND IS DELICIOUS REHEATED THE
FOLLOWING DAY.

Serves 6
Working time: about 1 hour
Total time: about 12 hours (includes marinating)

Calories **350**
Protein **37g.**
Cholesterol **75mg.**
Total fat **10g.**
Saturated fat **3g.**
Sodium **400mg.**

| |
|---|
| 1½ lb. beef top round, trimmed of fat and cut into 1-inch cubes |
| 1 cup white grape juice |
| ½ cup dry white wine |
| 2 tbsp. brandy |
| 1 tbsp. white wine vinegar |
| 1 large onion, sliced |
| 3 medium carrots, sliced |
| 1 large garlic clove, chopped |
| 1 bay leaf |
| 1 sprig rosemary |
| 3 or 4 sprigs thyme |
| 2 large sprigs parsley |
| 6 black peppercorns, lightly crushed |
| ½ tsp. salt |
| 2 to 3 tbsp. virgin olive oil |
| 2½ lb. ripe tomatoes (about 8 medium), peeled, seeded, and chopped, or two 14-oz. cans tomatoes, chopped |
| ½ lb. mushrooms, wiped clean and sliced |
| 1 strip orange zest |
| 2 oz. prosciutto, trimmed of excess fat and cut into strips |
| 12 black olives |

In a large bowl, combine the grape juice, wine, brandy, vinegar, onion, carrots, garlic, bay leaf, rosemary, thyme, parsley, peppercorns, and salt. Add the beef and mix the ingredients together. Cover the bowl and leave it in the refrigerator for 8 to 12 hours, stirring two or three times.

Preheat the oven to 300° F. Drain the meat, reserving the marinade, and pat the cubes dry with paper towels. Heat 1 tablespoon of the oil in a large, nonstick skillet over high heat. Add about one-third of the meat and cook until the pieces are well browned on all sides—two to three minutes. With a slotted spoon transfer the meat to a large, flameproof casserole. Brown the remaining beef in two batches in the same way, adding more oil to the skillet as necessary.

Pour the reserved marinade over the meat and add the chopped tomatoes. Stir together. Bring the mixture to a boil, cover the casserole tightly, and place it in the oven. Cook for two and a half hours.

Add the mushrooms, orange zest, prosciutto, and olives, and cook for 30 minutes more or until the beef is very tender. If there is a lot of excess liquid at this stage, cook uncovered.

SUGGESTED ACCOMPANIMENT: *green salad.*

## Spiced Chili Beef with Yogurt

THIS IS A VARIATION OF THE INDIAN CURRY *ROGHAN JOSH*. IT CAN BE MADE A DAY IN ADVANCE AND REHEATED.

Serves 4
Working time: about 1 hour and 15 minutes
Total time: about 3 hours and 30 minutes

Calories **295**
Protein **40g.**
Cholesterol **95mg.**
Total fat **12g.**
Saturated fat **6g.**
Sodium **265mg.**

| | |
|---|---|
| 1¼ lb. beef top round, trimmed of fat and cut into ¾-inch cubes | |
| 6 cardamom pods | |
| 2 tsp. coriander seeds | |
| 2 tsp. cumin seeds | |
| 2 tbsp. ghee or clarified butter, or 2 tbsp. safflower oil | |
| 1 medium onion, finely chopped | |
| 2 garlic cloves, crushed | |
| 2 fresh green chili peppers, finely chopped (cautionary note, page 8) | |
| 1-inch piece fresh ginger, peeled and crushed | |
| 2 tsp. ground turmeric | |
| 3 to 4 medium tomatoes, peeled and coarsely chopped | |
| ¼ tsp. salt | |
| ¾ cup plain low-fat yogurt (at room temperature) | |
| ½ small sweet red pepper, seeded, deribbed, and sliced into rings | |
| ½ small sweet green pepper, seeded, deribbed, and sliced into rings | |

Split the cardamom pods open and remove the seeds. Put the seeds into a heavy pan with the coriander and cumin seeds over moderate heat. Dry-fry for about five minutes, shaking the pan constantly until the seeds salt, and cook, stirring, for five minutes. Return the beef to the casserole and stir well to mix it in evenly with the other ingredients.

Reserve about 3 tablespoons of yogurt. Add the remainder to the casserole, 1 tablespoon at a time. Stir-fry after each addition until the yogurt is absorbed before adding the next spoonful—otherwise it will curdle. Cover the casserole with a double thickness of wax paper or foil and a lid. Cook in the oven for two hours until the meat is tender, stirring occasionally.

Just before serving, melt the remaining ghee, butter, or oil in a heavy skillet over moderately high heat, add the pepper rings, and toss for two to three minutes, until they are slightly softened. Drain them on paper towels. Transfer the contents of the casserole to a warmed serving dish, top with the pepper rings, and dribble the reserved yogurt over the top. Serve hot.

SUGGESTED ACCOMPANIMENTS: *nan bread; fresh spinach.*

*Beef & Pot Pie*

give off a spicy aroma ...
and crush them with a ...
aside until they are needed

Melt 2 table ...
... add on ...

... ... ... ... ... ... ... ...
... ... ... ... ... ... ... ...
... ... ... ... ... ... ... ...
... ... ... ... ... ... ... e-

Add ... ... ... ... ... ... to the casserole, and cook, ... ... ... ... tes more. Increase the heat, then add the tomatoes and

# Spicy Beef Stew with Apricots and Olives

Serves 8
Working time: about 30 minutes
Total time: about 2 hours and 30 minutes

Calories **290**
Protein **29g.**
Cholesterol **72mg.**
Total fat **11g.**
Saturated fat **3g.**
Sodium **275mg.**

| |
|---|
| 2½ lb. beef top round, trimmed of fat and cut into 1½-inch cubes |
| 1 tbsp. safflower oil |
| 3 onions, chopped |
| 4 garlic cloves, finely chopped |
| 14 oz. canned unsalted whole tomatoes, chopped, with their juice |
| 2 cups unsalted brown stock or unsalted chicken stock (recipes, page 138) |
| ½ cup red wine |
| 1½ tsp. ground cumin |
| 1½ tsp. ground coriander |
| ⅛ tsp. cayenne pepper |
| ¼ lb. dried apricot halves |
| 16 pitted green olives, rinsed and drained |

Heat the oil in a large, heavy-bottomed skillet over medium heat. Add the onions and cook them, stirring often, until they are translucent—about five minutes. With a slotted spoon, transfer the onions to a flame-proof casserole.

Increase the heat to medium high. Add the beef cubes to the skillet and brown them on all sides—five to seven minutes.

Transfer the beef to the casserole and add the garlic, the tomatoes and their juice, the stock, the wine, the cumin, the coriander, and the cayenne pepper. Cover the casserole, set it on top of the stove, and reduce the heat to low; simmer the beef, stirring occasionally, for one and a half hours.

Stir the apricots and olives into the casserole, and continue cooking the stew until the meat is tender—about 30 minutes more. Transfer the stew to a bowl or a deep platter, and serve.

SUGGESTED ACCOMPANIMENT: *rice tossed with scallions, currants, and sweet red pepper.*

# Bollito Misto

THIS LIGHTER VERSION OF THE CLASSIC ITALIAN BOILED DINNER
CALLS FOR COOKING THE BEEF GENTLY FOR
A LONG TIME. IF YOU LIKE, THE DISH MAY BE PREPARED
IN ADVANCE AND REHEATED.

Serves 16
Working time: about 1 hour and 15 minutes
Total time: about 6 hours

Calories **280**
Protein **33g.**
Cholesterol **90mg.**
Total fat **9g.**
Saturated fat **3g.**
Sodium **220mg.**

| |
|---|
| one 4-lb. arm pot roast, trimmed of fat |
| one 3-lb. chicken |
| 16 carrots, cut into 2½-inch lengths |
| 10 celery stalks, cut into 2½-inch lengths |
| 2 onions, quartered |
| 2 bay leaves |
| 8 black peppercorns |
| 2 sprigs fresh thyme, or ½ tsp. dried thyme leaves |
| 2 unpeeled garlic cloves |
| 16 white boiling onions |
| **Red sauce** |
| 28 oz. canned unsalted whole tomatoes, with their juice |
| 1 onion, finely chopped |
| 3 tbsp. cider vinegar |
| ¼ cup dry breadcrumbs |
| ¼ tsp. hot red-pepper flakes |
| **Green sauce** |
| ¾ cup dry breadcrumbs |
| 2 tsp. capers, rinsed |
| 2 tbsp. chopped fresh parsley |
| 3 garlic cloves |
| 2 anchovies, rinsed and patted dry |

Put the pot roast, about 1 cup each of the carrots and celery, the quartered onions, bay leaves, peppercorns, thyme, and garlic cloves into a large pot. Pour in enough water to cover them; bring the water to a simmer over medium-low heat. Cook the beef and vegetables for three hours.

Add the chicken to the pot and, if necessary, enough water to cover it. Continue to simmer the mixture until the chicken is tender and its juices run clear when a thigh is pierced with the tip of a sharp knife—about 45 minutes. Remove the beef and chicken from the pot and set them aside. Reserve the broth.

While the meats are cooking, make the accompanying sauces. For the red sauce, purée the tomatoes with their juice in a food processor or a blender. Strain the purée into a nonreactive saucepan, and add the onion, vinegar, breadcrumbs, and pepper flakes. Simmer the mixture, stirring occasionally, for 45 minutes. Pour the sauce into a bowl and refrigerate it.

For the green sauce, purée the breadcrumbs, capers, parsley, garlic, anchovies, and ¾ cup of the broth from the pot in a food processor or a blender. Pour the sauce into a small bowl and refrigerate it.

Skim the fat from the broth, then strain it through

a cheesecloth-lined sieve. Discard the solids. Rinse the pot; pour the broth back into it. Add the white onions and the remaining carrots and celery. Simmer the vegetables until they are tender—20 to 30 minutes.

Return the beef and chicken to the pot, cover the pot, and simmer them until they are heated through—about 15 minutes. Carve the beef and chicken, dis-carding the chicken skin. Arrange the pieces on a warm serving platter and moisten them with some of the broth. Save the rest of the broth for future use. Place the vegetables around the meat and serve immediately, with the sauces passed in separate bowls.

SUGGESTED ACCOMPANIMENT: *green salad*.

# Japanese Simmered Beef

THIS DISH IS A MEAL IN ITSELF. TRADITIONALLY, THE INGREDIENTS ARE PREPARED AND SERVED AT THE TABLE.

Serves 6
Working time: about 25 minutes
Total time: about 40 minutes

Calories **230**
Protein **20g.**
Cholesterol **37mg.**
Total fat **7g.**
Saturated fat **2g.**
Sodium **350mg.**

| |
|---|
| 1 lb. beef tenderloin, trimmed of fat and thinly sliced against the grain |
| ¼ lb. Japanese udon noodles or vermicelli |
| 1 large carrot, thinly sliced on the diagonal |
| 2 oz. fresh shiitake or other mushrooms, wiped clean, the stems discarded and the caps thinly sliced (about 1 cup) |
| 3 scallions, julienned |
| 1 cup Nappa cabbage, cut into chiffonade |
| ½ lb. tofu, cut into ¾-inch-wide strips |
| 6 cups unsalted brown stock or unsalted chicken stock (recipes, page 138), or a combination of both |
| 2 tbsp. low-sodium soy sauce |
| 2 tbsp. rice vinegar |
| 1 tsp. finely chopped fresh ginger |
| 1 tsp. finely chopped garlic |
| ¼ tsp. dark sesame oil |

Precook the noodles or vermicelli in 2 quarts of boiling water. Begin testing for doneness after five minutes and cook them until they are al dente. Drain the noodles in a colander and rinse them under running water to keep them from sticking together. Drain them again and set them aside in a bowl.

Arrange the tenderloin slices, carrot slices, mushrooms, scallions, cabbage, and tofu on a large plate.

Combine the stock, soy sauce, vinegar, ginger, and garlic in an electric skillet, a wok, or a fondue pot. Bring the mixture to a simmer and cook it for five minutes, then add the sesame oil.

Begin the meal by cooking pieces of the beef in the simmering broth. After the meat has been eaten, cook the vegetables and tofu in the broth until they are warmed through—three to four minutes. Finish the meal with the noodles or vermicelli, adding them to the broth and heating them through. They may be eaten with the broth or served on their own.

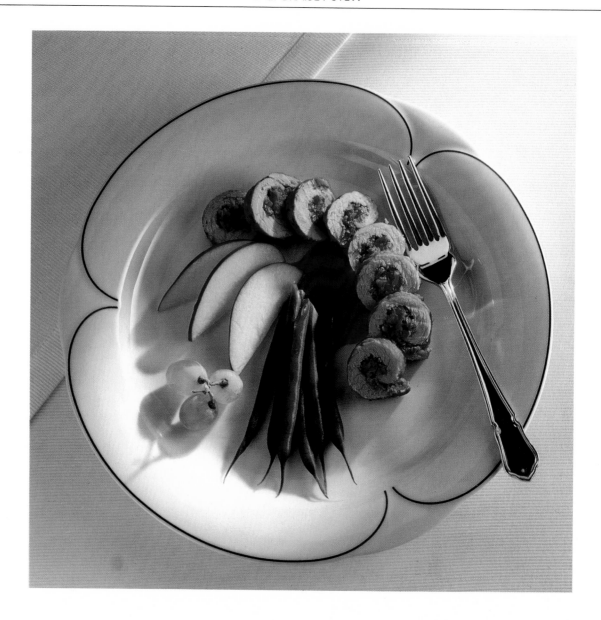

# Fruit-Stuffed Veal Olives

Serves 4
Working time: about 45 minutes
Total time: about 1 hour and 5 minutes

Calories **185**
Protein **18g.**
Cholesterol **80mg.**
Total fat **6g.**
Saturated fat **1g.**
Sodium **200mg.**

| |
|---|
| 4 veal cutlets (about 3 oz. each), trimmed of fat and flattened (page 32, Step 1) |
| 1 tbsp. safflower oil |
| about ⅔ cup grape juice |
| ½ tbsp. arrowroot |
| red apples, sliced, for garnish |
| seedless green grapes for garnish |
| **Spiced fruit stuffing** |
| ½ cup fresh cranberries, or ½ cup frozen cranberries, thawed |
| 1 tart red apple (about 5 oz.), quartered and cored |
| ¾ cup seedless green grapes |

| |
|---|
| 1½ tsp. freshly grated ginger |
| ½ tsp. pumpkin-pie spice |
| ½ tsp. salt |
| freshly ground black pepper |

First make the stuffing. Put the cranberries, apple quarters, grapes, and ginger into a food processor, and blend the ingredients until they are quite fine. Drain the fruit mixture in a fine sieve placed over a bowl to catch the juice, pressing down on the fruit to squeeze out all excess liquid; reserve the liquid. Add the pumpkin-pie spice, salt, and some pepper to the fruit mixture, and stir to blend. Spread one-quarter of the fruit mixture over each cutlet, then roll them up, tucking in the sides. Tie each roll with string.

Heat the oil in a small, nonstick skillet over medium-high heat. Add the veal rolls and brown them on all sides—about five minutes. As they are browned, transfer them to a saucepan in which they will fit comfortably. Add enough grape juice to the reserved fruit juice to make 1¼ cups. Pour this over the rolls and bring to a boil. Lower the heat, cover, and simmer the rolls for 20 minutes, turning them after 10 minutes.

Transfer the veal rolls to a cutting board. Slice the rolls, put them on a warmed serving dish, and keep them hot. Mix the arrowroot with a little cold water to make a smooth paste, then stir it into the cooking liquid. Simmer the mixture, stirring constantly, until it has thickened. Pour the sauce around the veal rolls and garnish with apple slices and grapes. Serve hot.

SUGGESTED ACCOMPANIMENT: *green beans.*

## Milanese-Style Braised Veal

Serves 6
Working time: about 40 minutes
Total time: about 2 hours and 45 minutes

Calories **290**
Protein **20g.**
Cholesterol **75mg.**
Total fat **10g.**
Saturated fat **3g.**
Sodium **210mg.**

| |
|---|
| 1¼ lb. veal top round, trimmed of fat and cut into ¾-inch cubes |
| 2 tbsp. virgin olive oil |
| 3 carrots, coarsely chopped |
| 2 celery stalks, trimmed and coarsely chopped |
| 1 onion, finely chopped |
| 2 garlic cloves, 1 crushed, 1 chopped |
| 2½ lb. ripe tomatoes (about 6), peeled, seeded, and chopped, or two 14-oz. cans plum tomatoes |
| ⅓ cup dry white wine |
| 2 bay leaves |
| 2 strips of lemon zest |
| 3 tbsp. finely chopped fresh mixed herbs (parsley, oregano, thyme) |
| ¼ tsp. salt |
| freshly ground black pepper |
| 1 lemon, grated zest only |

Heat 1 tablespoon of the oil in a flameproof casserole over high heat, add one-third of the veal, and brown the cubes on all sides, turning them constantly—about three minutes. With a slotted spoon, transfer the meat to a plate lined with paper towels. Repeat with the remaining two batches of veal, draining each batch on fresh towels.

Add the remaining oil to the casserole and lower the heat. Add the chopped carrots, celery, and onion to the casserole, stirring to scrape up the browned bits ▶

from the bottom of the pan. Cover the casserole with a lid, and cook the vegetables over the lowest possible heat for 10 minutes. Preheat the oven to 300° F.

Uncover the casserole, and add the crushed garlic, the veal, the tomatoes, the wine, the bay leaves, the strips of lemon zest, 1 tablespoon of the mixed herbs, the salt, and some pepper. Bring the mixture slowly to a boil, stirring, then cover with wax paper or foil and replace the lid. Braise the meat in the oven for two hours, or until the meat is tender, stirring occasionally to ensure even cooking.

Before serving, mix together the chopped garlic, the remaining herbs, and the grated lemon zest. Remove the bay leaves and strips of lemon zest from the casserole, transfer the contents of the casserole to a warmed serving dish, and sprinkle the garlic, herb, and lemon mixture over the top. Serve hot.

SUGGESTED ACCOMPANIMENT: *saffron rice.*

EDITOR'S NOTE: *This dish benefits from being left to stand overnight and reheated before serving; the flavors mellow and mature during this time.*

# Italian-Style Loin of Veal with Tuna Sauce

THIS RECIPE IS BASED ON THE CLASSIC *VITELLO TONNATO.* TOFU IS USED TO GIVE A SMOOTH, LOW-FAT SAUCE.

Serves 6
Working time: about 50 minutes
Total time: about 1 day and 5 hours (includes chilling)

Calories **270**
Protein **40g.**
Cholesterol **135mg.**
Total fat **10g.**
Saturated fat **3g.**
Sodium **260mg.**

| |
|---|
| one 2½-lb. loin of veal, boned, trimmed of fat, rolled and tied |
| 1 carrot, sliced |
| 1 celery stalk, sliced |
| 1 onion, sliced |
| 1 to 2 bay leaves |
| several sprigs rosemary and thyme |
| 1 small bunch parsley, tied with string |
| 8 black peppercorns |
| ⅛ tsp. salt |
| 3 cups unsalted chicken stock or unsalted veal stock (recipes, page 138) |
| **Tuna sauce** |
| 10 oz. tofu, drained |
| 1 tbsp. virgin olive oil |
| 2 tbsp. fresh lemon juice |
| 2 garlic cloves, crushed |
| ground white pepper |
| ½ cup canned tuna in water, drained and finely flaked |
| **Garnish** |
| 5 canned anchovy fillets, soaked in 6 tbsp. milk for 20 minutes, drained, rinsed, and patted dry |
| 1 to 2 tbsp. capers, drained |

Place the carrot, celery, and onion in the bottom of a heavy, flameproof casserole. Add the bay leaves, rosemary, thyme, parsley, peppercorns, and salt, then put the veal on top. Pour the stock around the meat and bring the liquid slowly to a boil. Lower the heat, cover the casserole, and poach gently until the veal feels tender when pierced in the center with a skewer—about one and a half hours. Remove the casserole from the heat and leave it covered in a cold place until the veal has cooled in the liquid.

When the veal is cool enough to handle, transfer it to a cutting board. Strain the stock into a bowl and return half of the liquid to the rinsed-out pan (reserve the rest for another use). Bring the stock to a boil and boil vigorously until it has reduced to 4 tablespoons—five to eight minutes. Set it aside to cool. Carve the meat into 12 neat slices and arrange them on a serving platter. Cover the platter loosely with aluminum foil and set the platter aside in a cold place.

To make the tuna sauce, purée the tofu in a blender or food processor with the oil, lemon juice, garlic, and some white pepper. Add the tuna and the reduced cooking liquid, and process the mixture until it has a smooth, coating consistency. Uncover the veal and coat it with the sauce, making sure that all the meat is covered. Cover the platter loosely with foil and chill it in the refrigerator for 24 hours to allow the flavor of the sauce to permeate the meat.

Remove the veal from the refrigerator about 30 minutes before serving time. Decorate it with the anchovies and capers.

SUGGESTED ACCOMPANIMENTS: *whole-grain bread; tomato and black olive salad.*

## Blanquette of Veal

Serves 4
Working time: about 50 minutes
Total time: about 2 hours

Calories **190**
Protein **20g**
Cholesterol **125mg.**
Total fat **7g.**
Saturated fat **3g.**
Sodium **250mg.**

| | |
|---|---|
| ¾ lb. veal top round or rump, trimmed of fat and cut into 1-inch cubes | |
| 8 white boiling onions or shallots | |
| 8 mushrooms, wiped clean | |
| 1 celery stalk, cut into chunks | |
| 1 sprig fresh thyme, or ½ tsp. dried thyme leaves | |
| 1 bay leaf | |
| 2 sprigs parsley | |
| 2½ cups unsalted veal stock or unsalted chicken stock (recipes, page 138) | |
| 8 small carrots | |
| 1 tbsp. cornstarch | |
| 1 cup low-fat milk | |
| 1 egg yolk | |
| 1 tbsp. lemon juice | |
| ½ tsp. salt | |
| ground white pepper | |

Put the veal into a heavy, medium-size saucepan and cover it with cold water. Bring the liquid to a boil, then drain. Return the veal to the pan, and add the onions or shallots, mushrooms, celery, thyme, bay leaf, parsley sprigs, and stock. Bring the mixture to a boil, lower the heat, cover, and simmer for 25 minutes. Add the carrots and simmer for 20 minutes more. Remove the veal and vegetables with a slotted spoon, and set them aside. Discard the herbs and strain the stock into a clean saucepan. Boil the stock to reduce it to 1¼ cups—10 to 15 minutes.

Dissolve the cornstarch in a little of the milk. Add the remaining milk to the stock and bring back to a boil. Lower the heat, whisk in the cornstarch mixture, and simmer for 10 minutes, stirring. Lightly beat the egg yolk with the lemon juice in a small bowl. Stir a little of the hot sauce into the egg yolk and lemon juice, and then stir this mixture into the remaining sauce in the pan. Cook gently, stirring, for one minute. Add the salt and some white pepper. Return the veal and vegetables to the sauce and heat through gently without boiling. Serve hot.

SUGGESTED ACCOMPANIMENTS: *boiled rice; peas.*

# Braised Veal

Serves 8
Working time: about 40 minutes
Total time: about 2 hours and 40 minutes

Calories **305**
Protein **33g.**
Cholesterol **90mg.**
Total fat **8g.**
Saturated fat **3g.**
Sodium **210mg.**

| |
|---|
| 2 to 2½ lb. veal top round, trimmed of fat and neatly tied |
| 1 tbsp. virgin olive oil |
| 2 onions, sliced |
| 4 carrots, coarsely sliced |
| 3 celery stalks, coarsely sliced |
| 1 leek, trimmed and coarsely sliced |
| ½ lb. rutabaga, diced |
| 1¼ cups unsalted veal stock or unsalted chicken stock (recipes, page 138) |
| ⅔ cup dry white wine |
| 2 garlic cloves |
| 2 bay leaves |
| several sprigs rosemary |
| several sprigs parsley |
| 1 tbsp. chopped fresh thyme, or 1 tsp. dried thyme leaves |
| ¼ tsp. salt |

Preheat the oven to 350° F. Heat the oil in a large, heavy-bottomed, nonreactive skillet over high heat. Brown the veal on all sides—about five minutes. Remove the veal from the pan and set it aside. Lower the heat, add the onions, carrots, celery, leek, and rutabaga to the oil remaining in the pan, and toss them gently until they glisten. Add the stock and wine, and bring to a boil. Transfer the vegetables and stock to an ovenproof casserole, place the veal on top of the vegetables, and add the garlic, bay leaves, rosemary, parsley, thyme, and salt. Cover the casserole with a tight-fitting lid or with aluminum foil.

Braise the veal in the oven for about two hours, basting frequently, until it is tender. When it is cooked, transfer the veal to a hot serving dish, remove the string, and cut it into slices. Discard the bay leaves and herbs. Using a slotted spoon, lift two-thirds of the vegetables, particularly the larger pieces, onto the serving dish. Cover them and keep them hot. Using a masher, mash the vegetables remaining in the stock. Bring the stock to a boil, then pour it into a hot pitcher or serving bowl. Serve with the veal.

SUGGESTED ACCOMPANIMENT: *creamed potatoes.*

# Tagine of Veal with Dried Fruit and Pine Nuts

*TAGINE* IS THE MOROCCAN WORD FOR AN EARTHENWARE COOKING POT—EXCELLENT FOR SLOW, MOIST OVEN COOKING, ESPECIALLY OF LEAN CUTS. FOR A SIMILAR EFFECT, YOU CAN USE AN ORDINARY CASSEROLE AND SEAL THE LID WITH A PASTE OF FLOUR AND WATER.

Serves 4
Working time: about 15 minutes
Total time: about 2 hours and 20 minutes

Calories **310**
Protein **29g.**
Cholesterol **75mg.**
Total fat **10g.**
Saturated fat **2g.**
Sodium **190mg.**

| |
|---|
| 1¼ lb. veal top round, trimmed of fat and cut into ¾-inch cubes |
| ½ large onion, finely chopped |
| 2½ tsp. paprika |
| 1½ tsp. ground ginger |
| ½ tsp. ground cinnamon |
| ⅛ tsp. salt |
| freshly ground black pepper |
| ⅓ cup dried apricots |
| ⅓ cup pitted prunes |
| ¼ cup pine nuts |
| 2 cups unsalted chicken stock or unsalted veal stock (recipes, page 138) |
| ⅛ tsp. saffron threads |
| cilantro sprigs for garnish |

Preheat the oven to 325° F. In a large bowl, mix together the veal, onion, paprika, ginger, cinnamon, salt, and some pepper, until the meat is evenly coated. Add the dried fruit and pine nuts, then transfer the mixture to the *tagine* or casserole.

Bring the stock to a boil and stir in the saffron. Pour it over the meat mixture, cover, and cook in the oven for two hours. Transfer to a serving bowl or serve hot, straight from the pot, garnished with cilantro.

SUGGESTED ACCOMPANIMENTS: *bulgur; plain yogurt.*

## Persian Veal and Bean Stew with Parsley

Serves 4
Working time: about 45 minutes
Total time: about 10 hours and 15 minutes
(includes soaking)

Calories **415**
Protein **35g.**
Cholesterol **105mg.**
Total fat **15g.**
Saturated fat **3g.**
Sodium **400mg.**

| |
|---|
| ¾ lb. veal top round or rump, trimmed of fat and ground or chopped (technique, page 15) |
| ⅔ cup dried chickpeas, soaked for 8 hours or overnight, drained |
| ⅔ cup dried red kidney beans, soaked for 8 hours or overnight, drained |
| 2 tbsp. safflower oil |
| 1 large onion, chopped |
| 1 garlic clove, finely chopped |
| 2 celery stalks, sliced |
| 2 cups loosely packed fresh parsley, stemmed and chopped |
| ¼ cup lemon juice |
| 2 cups unsalted veal stock or unsalted chicken stock (recipes, page 138) |
| 1 tsp. ground allspice |
| ¼ cup fresh whole-wheat breadcrumbs |
| ½ tsp. salt |
| freshly ground black pepper |

½ egg, beaten

Heat 1 tablespoon of the oil in a 12-inch diameter, shallow, flameproof casserole. Add the onion, garlic, celery, and two-thirds of the parsley. Cover and cook over low heat, stirring occasionally, for about 10 minutes, or until the vegetables are softened. Add the chickpeas, lemon juice, half of the stock, and the allspice, and stir to mix. Bring to a boil, cover again, and simmer for 30 minutes. Stir in the kidney beans with half of the remaining stock. Cover again and simmer for 30 minutes.

Meanwhile, combine the veal, breadcrumbs, remaining parsley, ¼ teaspoon of the salt, and some pepper in a bowl. Work the ingredients together with your hands, and add enough egg to bind them. Divide the mixture into 12 equal portions and shape them into balls. Heat the remaining oil in a nonstick skillet over medium-high heat. Add the meatballs and brown them on all sides, turning them and shaking the pan so that they color evenly—about five minutes.

Add the meatballs to the bean stew. Add the remaining salt and some pepper. Simmer, covered, for one hour more or until the beans are tender, stirring occasionally and adding a little extra stock if necessary.

SUGGESTED ACCOMPANIMENT: *a salad of Belgian endive and orange sections.*

*4 A phyllo parcel, baked to a rich gold, is sliced to reveal the beef tenderloin within (recipe, opposite).*

# A Medley of Ideas

## Beef Tenderloin Wrapped in Phyllo

Many of the new, light beef and veal dishes do not fall neatly into the traditional categories of roasting, broiling, sautéing, or braising. This chapter presents an array of dishes, from grills to pâtés, that reveal the range of opportunities open to the imaginative, health-conscious cook.

Some of the recipes call for ground beef or veal, long the basis of many familiar dishes prepared on a family budget. However, the fatty meat usually found at the supermarket is replaced with the leanest cuts, custom-ground by the butcher or hand-chopped at home. Thus, the fat content stays low while the economical, meat-stretching appeal of such favorites as meat loaf and stuffed peppers is retained with the use of savory vegetable and grain fillers.

In many of the dishes, the meat and its complementary spices, herbs, or vegetables are sautéed together, then baked with other ingredients. This combination of techniques is one of the kitchen's happiest marriages, adding the flavor contributed by browning to the handsome appearance of a baked dish. On page 116, for example, ground beef is precooked with tomatoes, onion, green pepper, and spices, then baked in a corn bread batter that rises to surround the meat in a tender, golden crust.

Baked dishes provide inspired contrasts and combinations: beef tenderloin wrapped in phyllo *(recipe, right)*, silky mashed potatoes covering beef cooked with shallots and apples *(page 112)*, or beef cooked in a yogurt and egg custard garnished with almonds *(page 119)*. And baking can transform ground or diced veal into dishes of great refinement; both the veal pâté with peaches and peppercorns *(page 120)* and the veal terrine with spinach, cheese, and juniper berries *(page 122)* would make an excellent first course for a lunch or dinner party. As with all the recipes in the chapter, the calorie and fat content are moderate, yet flavor and texture have not been compromised.

Serves 8
Working time: about 40 minutes
Total time: about 3 hours and 15 minutes
(includes marinating)

Calories **300**
Protein **32g.**
Cholesterol **65mg.**
Total fat **12g.**
Saturated fat **4g.**
Sodium **75mg.**

| |
|---|
| one 2½-lb. piece beef tenderloin, fully trimmed and neatly tied |
| 3 tbsp. virgin olive oil |
| 1 tsp. mixed dried herbs |
| 1 garlic clove, crushed |
| freshly ground black pepper |
| ¼ cup red wine |
| 1 onion, finely chopped |
| ½ lb. mushrooms, wiped clean, trimmed, and chopped |
| 2 tbsp. chopped fresh parsley |
| 7 oz. phyllo pastry (about 7 sheets, each 12 by 18 inches) |
| 1 tbsp. unsalted butter, melted |
| cooked mushrooms for garnish (optional) |

In a shallow dish, blend 1 tablespoon of the oil with the herbs, garlic, and pepper. Add the beef and turn it in the marinade until it is evenly coated. Cover it and marinate at room temperature for at least one hour.

Heat another tablespoon of the oil in a large, non-stick sauté pan or skillet over high heat. Brown the beef on all sides—about five to eight minutes—then transfer it to a plate. Strain off all the fat from the pan and stir in 2 tablespoons of the wine. Bring the liquid to a boil and boil until reduced by half—about one minute. Pour it over the beef and set the meat aside until cold.

Meanwhile, heat the remaining oil in the pan, add the onion, and cook it over low heat for five to six minutes until it is softened but not browned. Add the mushrooms and cook until they are softened—six to eight minutes. Stir the remaining wine into the mushrooms, bring to a boil, and cook until all the juices in the pan have evaporated—about five minutes. Stir in the parsley. Set aside to cool.

Heat the oven to 450° F. Lay the pastry sheets out flat, one on top of another, and cut a 2-inch-wide strip from one side. Cut the strip into diamond shapes *(overleaf, Steps 1 and 2)*. Fill the pastry with the mushroom mixture and tenderloin, then make a parcel, and glaze and decorate it *(overleaf, Steps 3 through 6)*.

Bake for 35 minutes or until golden brown. Remove to a serving dish and garnish with the mushrooms, if desired. Cut into thick slices and serve immediately.

SUGGESTED ACCOMPANIMENT: *new potatoes with chives.*

# Making a Light Pastry Parcel

**1** *PREPARING THE DECORATION. Take seven 12-by-18-inch sheets of phyllo pastry and stack them on top of each other on a flat surface. With a sharp knife, trim off two 2-inch strips from one short side. To make the strips as even as possible, hold the pastry in place with one hand while you cut.*

**2** *CUTTING THE DECORATION. Cut across the two pastry strips diagonally to make diamond shapes. Set the pieces aside for use later as decoration, covering them with a damp dishtowel to keep them from drying out.*

**3** *ASSEMBLING THE PARCEL. Spread the mushroom mixture lengthwise down the center of the uncut phyllo to form a rectangle approximately the length and width of the tenderloin, and lay the meat on top of the mushroom mixture. Fold the short sides of the phyllo over the ends of the beef.*

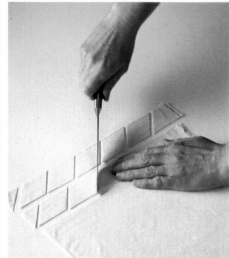

**4** *WRAPPING THE PARCEL. Fold the two long sides of the phyllo pastry over the tenderloin. Press the pastry firmly against the beef to create a neat, secure parcel.*

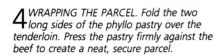

**5** *GLAZING WITH BUTTER. Turn the parcel over and place it, seam side down, on a nonstick baking sheet. Brush the exposed surface of the pastry lightly with melted unsalted butter. This glazing will hold the decoration in place and cause the pastry to turn a rich golden brown when it is baked.*

**6** *DECORATING THE PARCEL. Arrange the reserved seven-layer phyllo diamonds in two overlapping rows running the length of the beef parcel, to resemble a spray of leaves. Brush the phyllo diamonds lightly with melted unsalted butter.*

# Sirloin-Filled Pita Sandwiches

Serves 6
Working (and total) time: about 1 hour and 15 minutes

Calories **300**
Protein **22g.**
Cholesterol **38mg.**
Total fat **11g.**
Saturated fat **3g.**
Sodium **205mg.**

| |
|---|
| ¾ lb. sirloin steak, trimmed of fat and thinly sliced |
| 1 red onion, thickly sliced |
| 6 whole-wheat pita breads |
| ¼ lb. part-skim mozzarella, grated |
| 3 garlic cloves, finely chopped |
| 12 Kalamata olives or black olives, pitted and chopped |
| 2 large ripe tomatoes, each cut into 6 slices |
| 1 tbsp. safflower oil |

Put the onion slices on the rack of a broiler pan and broil them until they are soft—about four minutes. Remove the onions from the rack and set them aside. Lay the slices of meat on the rack and broil them until they are browned—about two minutes in all.

Split a pita bread into two rounds. On the bottom half, layer one-sixth of the onion, beef, cheese, garlic, olives, and tomatoes. Set the top half in place. Repeat the process to make five more sandwiches.

Lightly brush the outside of the sandwiches with the oil. Toast the sandwiches in a waffle iron or in a skillet over medium heat until the bread is crisp and brown and the cheese has melted—about four minutes. Cut each sandwich in two before serving.

# Beef and Potato Pie

Serves 4
Working time: about 1 hour
Total time: about 2 hours

| | |
|---|---|
| Calories **485**<br>Protein **32g.**<br>Cholesterol **72mg.**<br>Total fat **12g.**<br>Saturated fat **3g.**<br>Sodium **270mg.** | 1¼ lb. beef round, trimmed of fat and ground<br>or chopped (technique, page 15) |
| | 2 lb. potatoes, peeled and quartered |
| | 2 tbsp. skim milk |
| | 2 tbsp. chopped fresh parsley |
| | ¼ tsp. salt |
| | 4 tsp. safflower oil |
| | 3 tbsp. unbleached all-purpose flour |
| | 2 cups unsalted brown stock or unsalted<br>chicken stock (recipes, page 138) |
| | 1 cup thinly sliced shallots or onions |
| | 1 cup dried apples, chopped |
| | 2 tbsp. cider vinegar |
| | 1 tbsp. chopped fresh thyme, or 1 tsp.<br>dried thyme leaves |
| | freshly ground black pepper |

Preheat the oven to 450° F.

Place the potatoes in a saucepan and add enough water to cover them. Bring the water to a boil, then lower the heat and simmer the potatoes until they are tender—15 to 20 minutes. Drain the potatoes, spread them out on a baking sheet, and place them in the oven to dry. After five minutes, remove the pan from the oven, and purée the potatoes by working them through a sieve or a food mill set over a bowl. Combine the potatoes with the milk, chopped parsley, and salt, and set them aside.

Blend 2 teaspoons of the oil and all of the flour in a saucepan over low heat, and cook the paste for one minute. Gradually whisk in the stock and simmer the

# Beet Hamburgers

Serves 8
Working time: about 20 minutes
Total time: about 2 hours

| | |
|---|---|
| Calories **320**<br>Protein **31g.**<br>Cholesterol **71mg.**<br>Total fat **10g.**<br>Saturated fat **3g.**<br>Sodium **310mg.** | 2½ lb. beef round, trimmed of fat and ground<br>or chopped (technique, page 15) |
| | 2 lb. beets, washed, all but 1 inch of the stems cut off |
| | 1 small onion, peeled and grated |
| | 8 cornichons, chopped, or 2 small dill pickles, chopped |
| | ¼ cup dry breadcrumbs |
| | ¼ cup distilled white vinegar |
| | freshly ground black pepper |
| | 2 tsp. safflower oil |
| | ½ cup unsalted brown stock or unsalted<br>chicken stock (recipes, page 138) |
| | 1 tsp. caraway seeds |
| | 8 onion rolls, split |

Preheat the oven to 400° F. Wrap all the beets together in a single package of aluminum foil and bake them until they are tender—approximately one hour. Unwrap the beets and let them cool. Peel and grate the beets. Put ½ cup of the beets into a large bowl, and set the remainder aside.

Add the ground beef, onion, cornichons or dill pickles, breadcrumbs, vinegar, and some pepper to the bowl. Mix the ingredients thoroughly, then shape the mixture into eight patties.

Heat the oil in a large, nonstick skillet over medium-high heat. Add the patties to the skillet and brown them for about one minute per side. Add the reserved beets, the stock, the caraway seeds, and some pepper. Cover the skillet and reduce the heat to medium low. Simmer the mixture for 20 minutes.

Serve the hamburgers in the onion rolls, with the beets alongside.

SUGGESTED ACCOMPANIMENT: *cucumbers with dill.*

mixture slowly over low heat until it thickens—about two minutes. Remove the pan from the heat.

Place the shallots or onions, apples, and vinegar in a heavy-bottomed, nonreactive skillet, and cook them over medium heat until the vinegar has evaporated and the shallots or onions are limp—about two minutes. Add the beef and brown it over high heat, breaking up any whole pieces as you do so. Remove the skillet from the heat, and stir in the thyme, some pepper, and the thickened stock.

Divide the meat mixture evenly among four small gratin dishes, or place it in one large dish. Top the meat with the potato mixture, smooth the surface with a spatula, and flute the potatoes, using the edge of the spatula. Brush the surface with the remaining 2 teaspoons of oil. Bake the beef and potatoes until the potatoes are lightly browned—20 to 30 minutes.

SUGGESTED ACCOMPANIMENT: *Bibb lettuce and radish salad.*

# Ground Beef with Peppers and Pasta

Serves 6
Working (and total) time: about 45 minutes

Calories **415**
Protein **28g.**
Cholesterol **50mg.**
Total fat **9g.**
Saturated fat **3g.**
Sodium **260mg.**

| |
|---|
| 1¼ lb. beef round, trimmed of fat and ground or chopped (technique, page 15) |
| 2 sweet red peppers |
| 1 tbsp. virgin olive oil |
| 2 onions, finely chopped |
| 1 tsp. fennel seeds |
| 6 garlic cloves, thinly sliced |
| 1 tsp. salt |
| freshly ground black pepper |
| 14 oz. canned unsalted whole tomatoes, drained, seeded, and chopped, the juice reserved |
| ⅓ cup red wine vinegar |
| 1 tsp. sugar |
| 2 zucchini (about ¾ lb.), trimmed, halved lengthwise, and cut on the diagonal into ¼-inch pieces |
| ¾ lb. penne or other tubular pasta |
| 1 cup unsalted chicken stock (recipe, page 138) |
| ½ cup tightly packed fresh basil leaves, shredded |
| ¼ cup freshly grated Parmesan cheese |

Roast the peppers about 2 inches below a preheated broiler, turning them every now and then until their skins become blistered. Transfer the peppers to a bowl and cover it with plastic wrap; the trapped steam will make the peppers limp and loosen their skins. When the peppers are cool, peel, seed, and derib them, holding them over a bowl to catch any juice. Cut the peppers into thin strips and strain the juice to remove any seeds. Set the strips and juice aside.

While the peppers are roasting, heat the oil in a heavy-bottomed, nonreactive skillet over medium-high heat. Add the ground beef, chopped onions, fennel seeds, garlic, ¼ teaspoon of the salt, and some pepper. Cook the mixture, stirring frequently, until the beef begins to brown. Add the tomatoes and their juice, the red wine vinegar, and the sugar. Reduce the heat to medium low and simmer the mixture for 10 minutes. Add the zucchini and the pepper strips and their juice; cook the mixture for five minutes more.

Meanwhile, add the pasta and the remaining ¾ teaspoon salt to 3 quarts of boiling water; cook the pasta for six minutes—it will be underdone. Drain the pasta and return it to the pot; pour in the stock, cover the pot, and slowly bring the stock to a simmer. Cook the pasta for one minute longer, then add the beef mixture, the basil, and a liberal grinding of pepper, and stir well. Simmer the mixture, stirring frequently, until most of the liquid is absorbed—two to three minutes.

Transfer the beef and pasta to a large bowl. Sprinkle the Parmesan cheese over the top and serve at once.

SUGGESTED ACCOMPANIMENT: *arugula or other salad greens.*

# Spicy Ground Beef on a Bed of Sweet Potatoes

Serves 4
Working time: about 1 hour
Total time: about 2 hours and 30 minutes

Calories **522**
Protein **35g.**
Cholesterol **73mg.**
Total fat **10g.**
Saturated fat **3g.**
Sodium **260mg.**

| |
|---|
| 1¼ lb. beef round, trimmed of fat and ground or chopped (technique, page 15) |
| 4 sweet potatoes (about 2¼ lb.) |
| 3 lb. ripe tomatoes, chopped |
| 2 bay leaves |
| 2 cinnamon sticks |
| 4 whole allspice |
| 8 black peppercorns |
| 2 dried red chili peppers (cautionary note, page 8), or ¼ tsp. cayenne pepper |
| 1 tbsp. tomato paste |
| 1 tsp. safflower oil |
| 1 onion, finely chopped |
| ¼ tsp. salt |
| 2 tbsp. chopped fresh parsley |
| ½ cup low-fat yogurt |

Preheat the oven to 400° F. Bake the sweet potatoes for one hour, or until they are tender when pierced with the tip of a sharp knife.

Meanwhile, put the tomatoes, bay leaves, cinnamon sticks, whole allspice, peppercorns, and chili peppers or cayenne pepper into a heavy-bottomed, nonreactive pan. Bring the mixture to a boil, then reduce the heat to medium low and simmer it uncovered, stirring frequently, until it is reduced to 2 cups—about one hour and 30 minutes. Remove the cinnamon sticks and bay leaves from the tomato sauce, discard them, and put the sauce through a food mill. Set the sauce aside.

Sauté the beef in a large, nonstick skillet over high heat, breaking it into chunks as it cooks. When the beef is evenly browned—about five minutes—add the tomato sauce and the tomato paste. Simmer the meat, partially covered to prevent spattering, until most of the liquid has evaporated—about 20 minutes. Pour the meat sauce into a bowl and keep it warm.

Peel the baked sweet potatoes and chop them coarsely. Wipe out the skillet with a paper towel, pour in the oil, and heat it over low heat. Add the onion and cook it until it is translucent—about five minutes. Add the sweet potatoes and ¼ cup of water, and cook the mixture, stirring frequently, over medium heat until the water is absorbed—about five minutes. Stir in the salt and the chopped parsley.

Place the sweet potatoes on a serving platter and top them with the meat. Serve immediately, passing the yogurt separately.

SUGGESTED ACCOMPANIMENT: *steamed snow peas.*

# Bulgur-Stuffed Red Peppers

Serves 4
Working time: about 35 minutes
Total time: about 1 hour

Calories **285**
Protein **20g.**
Cholesterol **40mg.**
Total fat **9g.**
Saturated fat **2g.**
Sodium **210mg.**

| |
| --- |
| ¾ lb. beef round, trimmed of fat and ground or chopped (technique, page 15) |
| 4 large sweet red or green peppers |
| 4 tsp. virgin olive oil |
| 1 onion, chopped |
| 2 tsp. chopped fresh thyme, or ½ tsp. dried thyme leaves |
| ¼ lb. mushrooms, wiped clean and thinly sliced (about 1¼ cups) |
| 2 tbsp. finely chopped celery |
| ¾ cup bulgur |
| ¼ tsp. salt |
| freshly ground black pepper |
| 1½ cups unsalted brown stock or unsalted chicken stock (recipes, page 138) |
| 1 garlic clove, finely chopped |
| 2 tbsp. sherry vinegar or red wine vinegar |

Preheat the oven to 400° F.

To prepare the peppers, cut out and discard their stems. Slice off the peppers' tops, dice them, and set the pieces aside. Seed and derib the peppers.

Heat 1 tablespoon of the oil in a heavy-bottomed saucepan over medium heat. Add half of the onion, half of the thyme, all of the mushrooms, celery, bulgur, ⅛ teaspoon of the salt, and some pepper. Cook the vegetables and bulgur, stirring frequently, for five minutes. Add the stock, stir the mixture well, and cover the pan. Cook the mixture, stirring it occasionally, until the liquid is absorbed—about 12 minutes.

In a heavy-bottomed, nonstick skillet, heat the remaining teaspoon of oil over medium-high heat. When the skillet is hot, add the beef, the reserved diced pepper tops, the remaining onion, the remaining thyme, and the garlic. Cook, stirring frequently, until the beef is browned—five to seven minutes. Add the remaining ⅛ teaspoon of salt, some pepper, and the

vinegar. Cook the mixture for 30 seconds, then remove it from the heat.

Combine the bulgur mixture with the beef and fill the peppers, mounding the filling. Bake the stuffed peppers in a shallow casserole, loosely covered with aluminum foil, for 25 minutes. Allow the peppers to stand for five minutes before serving them.

SUGGESTED ACCOMPANIMENT: *cucumber and onion salad.*

bring the liquid to a simmer over medium heat. Lower the heat, cover the pan, leaving the lid slightly ajar, and simmer the mixture, stirring occasionally, for one hour and 30 minutes. If the tomato sauce begins to scorch, stir about ½ cup of water into it.

While the meat is cooking, make the cabbage slaw. Toss the cabbage in a bowl with the carrot, apple, yogurt, mustard, horseradish, salt, and celery seeds. Cover the bowl and refrigerate it.

When the meat is done, remove it from the saucepan and let it sit at room temperature. Add the celery leaves, lemon juice, brown sugar, hot red-pepper sauce, salt, and some pepper to the tomato sauce. Coarsely chop the beef and add it also. Simmer the beef barbecue over low heat for 30 minutes.

Split the rolls and fill them with the beef, topped with some of the cabbage slaw.

## Beef Barbecue Sandwiches

Serves 8
Working time: about 45 minutes
Total time: about 2 hours and 30 minutes

Calories **380**
Protein **34g.**
Cholesterol **87mg.**
Total fat **10g.**
Saturated fat **3g.**
Sodium **435mg.**

| |
|---|
| one 2½ lb. arm pot roast, trimmed of fat |
| 28 oz. canned unsalted whole tomatoes, puréed in a food processor or a blender, and sieved |
| 1 onion, finely chopped |
| ¾ cup cider vinegar |
| ½ cup finely chopped celery leaves |
| juice of 1 lemon |
| ¼ cup light brown sugar |
| 10 drops hot red-pepper sauce |
| ¼ tsp. salt |
| freshly ground black pepper |
| 8 kaiser rolls |
| **Cabbage slaw** |
| ½ small head of cabbage, shredded (about 4 cups) |
| 1 small carrot, grated |
| 1 red apple, grated |
| 1 cup low-fat yogurt |
| ½ tsp. dry mustard |
| 1 tsp. prepared horseradish |
| ¼ tsp. salt |
| ½ tsp. celery seeds |

First simmer the beef in a tomato sauce. Place the puréed tomatoes in a large, nonreactive saucepan with 3 cups of water. Add the onion, vinegar, and beef, and

## Spicy Ground Beef Baked in Corn Bread

Serves 4
Working time: about 25 minutes
Total time: about 1 hour

Calories **395**
Protein **28g.**
Cholesterol **56mg.**
Total fat **10g.**
Saturated fat **3g.**
Sodium **325mg.**

| |
|---|
| 1 lb. beef round, trimmed of fat, ground or chopped (technique, page 15), and crumbled into small pieces |
| 1 onion, chopped |
| ½ sweet green pepper, seeded, deribbed, and diced |
| 3 garlic cloves, thinly sliced |
| 1 tsp. chili powder |
| 1 tsp. dry mustard |
| ¼ tsp. cayenne pepper |
| 14 oz. canned unsalted whole tomatoes, drained |
| 1 tsp. sugar |
| ⅓ cup red wine vinegar |
| ⅛ tsp. salt |
| **Corn bread** |
| ⅔ cup yellow stone-ground cornmeal |
| ⅔ cup unbleached all-purpose flour |
| 1 tbsp. sugar |
| 1½ tsp. baking powder |
| ½ tsp. chili powder |
| 1 tbsp. safflower oil |
| ¾ cup low-fat milk |
| 1 egg white |

Heat a large, nonstick skillet over medium-high heat. Combine the beef, onion, green pepper, garlic, chili powder, mustard, and cayenne pepper in the skillet. Stir the mixture frequently, until the beef is cooked through—four to five minutes. Add the tomatoes, sugar, vinegar, and salt, crushing the tomatoes. Cook the mixture until most of the liquid has evaporated—15 to 20 minutes. Set it aside.

Preheat the oven to 450° F.

To make the corn bread, sift the cornmeal, flour, sugar, baking powder, and chili powder into a bowl. Add the oil, stir well, and work the oil into the dry ingredients with your fingertips until no lumps remain; the mixture will be very dry.

In a separate bowl, beat the milk and the egg white together, and add this to the cornmeal mixture. Stir gently just to incorporate the liquid into the dry ingredients; do not overmix.

Lightly oil a 1½-quart baking dish. Pour the corn-bread batter into the dish. Spoon the beef and vegetables into the center of the batter, leaving a 1½-inch border all around. Bake the mixture for 25 minutes. Remove the dish from the oven and let it stand for five minutes before serving.

SUGGESTED ACCOMPANIMENT: *red-pepper and scallion salad.*

## Steak and Chestnut Pie

Serves 6
Working time: about 45 minutes
Total time: about 2 hours and 45 minutes
(includes cooling)

Calories **300**
Protein **21g.**
Cholesterol **45mg.**
Total fat **20g.**
Saturated fat **5g.**
Sodium **140mg.**

| |
|---|
| 1 lb. beef rump steak, trimmed of fat and cut into 1-inch cubes |
| 1 onion, sliced |
| ⅓ cup fresh orange juice |
| ½ cup brown stock (recipe, page 138) |
| ½ orange, grated zest only |
| 1 cup peeled fresh chestnuts, or ½ cup dried chestnuts, soaked overnight and drained |
| 1 tbsp. tomato paste |
| 1 tsp. chopped fresh thyme, or ¼ tsp. dried thyme leaves |
| freshly ground black pepper |
| ⅛ tsp. salt |
| 6 carrots, sliced |
| 4 celery stalks, cut diagonally into 1-inch slices |
| ½ lb. mushrooms, wiped clean |

| |
|---|
| 1 to 2 tbsp. skim milk to glaze |
| **Crust** |
| 1½ cups unbleached all-purpose flour |
| 1½ tsp. baking powder |
| ½ tsp. dry mustard |
| ⅛ tsp. salt |
| 6 tbsp. solid vegetable shortening, well chilled |

Put the steak and sliced onion into a heavy, flameproof casserole, and add the orange juice and stock. Bring the liquid to a boil, then add the orange zest, chestnuts, tomato paste, thyme, pepper, and salt. Lower the heat, cover, and simmer for 30 minutes. Add the carrots and celery, and simmer for 30 minutes more. Remove the casserole from the heat, stir in the mushrooms, and turn the contents into a 9-inch glass or ceramic pie pan. Let the beef cool.

To make the crust, preheat the oven to 400° F. Sift the flour, baking powder, mustard, and salt into a bowl. Add the vegetable shortening, and using two knives, cut the shortening into the flour just long enough to produce a fine-meal texture. With a fork, mix in ½ to ⅔ cup of cold water to make a soft but not sticky dough. Knead lightly until just smooth.

Roll out the pastry on a floured surface until it is 1 inch larger than the top of the pie pan. Cut ½-inch-wide strips from the edge of the pastry and press them onto the dampened rim of the pie pan, to hold the top crust in place. Dampen the pastry rim and lift the large piece of pastry on top of the pie. Press together to seal, trim the edge, and crimp it. Make a hole in the center.

Brush the pastry with skim milk. Decorate it with pastry trimmings, and brush these also with the milk. Place the pie pan on a baking sheet and bake for 45 minutes, or until the pastry is golden brown. Serve hot, straight from the pan.

SUGGESTED ACCOMPANIMENT: *a green vegetable such as broccoli, Brussels sprouts, or cabbage.*

# Bobotie

Serves 8
Working time: about 40 minutes
Total time: about 2 hours

Calories **270**
Protein **28g.**
Cholesterol **100mg.**
Total fat **10g.**
Saturated fat **3g.**
Sodium **260mg.**

| |
|---|
| 1½ lb. beef top round, trimmed of fat and ground or chopped (technique, page 15) |
| 5 tsp. safflower oil |
| 2 onions, chopped |
| 1 garlic clove, crushed |
| 2 tsp. turmeric |
| 2 tsp. ground cumin |
| 2 tsp. ground coriander |
| 1 tsp. chili powder |
| 1 tsp. ground cinnamon |
| 1 tsp. ground ginger |
| ½ tsp. salt |
| freshly ground black pepper |
| 6 tbsp. golden raisins |
| 6 tbsp. raisins |
| ¼ cup cider vinegar |
| 1 scant cup fresh whole-wheat breadcrumbs |
| ⅔ cup skim milk |
| ⅔ cup plain low-fat yogurt |
| 2 eggs, beaten |
| ⅓ cup sliced almonds |
| 4 to 6 small bay leaves |

Heat 4 teaspoons of the oil in a small, nonstick skillet over medium heat. Cook the onion and garlic in the oil until they are softened—about five minutes. Add the ▶

turmeric, cumin, coriander, chili powder, cinnamon, ginger, salt, and some pepper, and cook, stirring, for 30 seconds. Transfer the mixture to a large bowl. Add the ground beef, golden raisins, raisins, and vinegar.

Preheat the oven to 350° F. Put the breadcrumbs and milk into a small bowl, and stir together with a fork. Drain the crumbs in a sieve over a bowl and reserve the milk, pressing the crumbs to extract all excess liquid. Add the breadcrumbs to the beef mixture, and work the ingredients together with your hands until they are thoroughly amalgamated.

Use the remaining teaspoon of oil to grease a deep, 3-quart, flameproof dish. Pack the beef mixture into the dish and smooth the surface.

Mix the reserved milk with the yogurt and beaten eggs, and pour it over the meat mixture. Scatter the almonds over the top and decorate with the bay leaves. Bake for one and a quarter hours, or until the topping is set and golden brown. Serve hot.

SUGGESTED ACCOMPANIMENT: *a salad of oakleaf lettuce and curly endive.*

## Veal, Peach, and Peppercorn Pâté

Serves 8
Working time: about 30 minutes
Total time: 1½ to 2 days (includes marinating and chilling)

Calories **250**
Protein **13g.**
Cholesterol **75mg.**
Total fat **4g.**
Saturated fat **2g.**
Sodium **200mg.**

| |
|---|
| 1 lb. veal top round, trimmed of fat and cut into 1-inch dice |
| ½ cup dried peaches, diced |
| ½ cup dry white wine |
| 30 fresh green peppercorns, 10 crushed |
| 1 scant cup fresh whole-wheat breadcrumbs |
| 1 lemon, finely grated zest and juice |
| 2 tbsp. brandy |
| 1 egg, beaten |
| ¼ tsp. ground allspice |
| ⅛ tsp. salt |
| lemon wedges for garnish (optional) |
| fresh green peppercorn sprigs for garnish (optional) |
| **Peach sauce** |
| ¼ cup dried peaches |
| ⅓ cup dry white wine |
| ⅛ tsp. ground allspice |

Place the diced veal, peaches, and wine in a bowl, cover, and let the ingredients marinate in a cold place or the refrigerator for 24 hours, turning occasionally.

Preheat the oven to 325° F. Put the veal, peaches, and any remaining liquid into a food processor, chop finely, and then transfer the mixture to a large bowl. Add the whole and crushed peppercorns, bread-crumbs, grated lemon zest and juice, brandy, egg, allspice, and salt. Mix thoroughly.

Line the bottom of a 4-cup loaf pan with dampened wax paper. Pack the pâté mixture into the pan and smooth the surface. Cover with foil, set the loaf pan in a roasting pan, and pour in enough boiling water to come halfway up the sides of the loaf pan. Cook in the oven for one hour. Remove the loaf pan from the water and let the pâté cool.

When it is cool, take off the foil, cover the surface of the pâté with dampened wax paper, and weight it down with unopened cans or scale weights set on top of a board. Chill the pâté in the refrigerator for eight hours or overnight.

To make the peach sauce, put the dried peaches into a heavy-bottomed, nonreactive saucepan, add 2 cups of water and the wine, and bring to a boil. Cover the pan and simmer the peaches over very low heat until they are tender—about 30 minutes. Transfer the peaches and their cooking liquid to a food processor, and blend until smooth. Pour the purée into a mixing bowl, add ½ cup of water and the allspice, and whisk the mixture vigorously. Let the sauce cool, then chill it in the refrigerator until serving time.

To serve, turn the pâté out of the pan and cut it into 16 thin slices. Arrange two slices on individual plates, and garnish each serving with a lemon wedge and a green peppercorn sprig, if desired. Whisk the sauce, adding, if necessary, a few spoonfuls of water or wine to thin it down. Pour the sauce into a gravy boat or small bowl, and pass it separately.

SUGGESTED ACCOMPANIMENT: *grated celeriac tossed in a little mayonnaise and lemon juice.*

# Hot Veal and Spinach Terrine

Serves 8 as a first course, 4 as a main course
Working time: about 30 minutes
Total time: about 1 hour and 40 minutes

Calories **130**
Protein **16g.**
Cholesterol **80mg.**
Total fat **6g.**
Saturated fat **2g.**
Sodium **260mg.**

| |
|---|
| *1 lb. veal top round, trimmed of fat and diced* |
| *¾ lb. spinach leaves, coarse stems removed, washed* |
| *¼ tsp. freshly grated or ground nutmeg* |
| *¼ tsp. salt* |
| *4 oz. low-fat cream cheese* |
| *2 tbsp. heavy cream* |
| *1 egg* |
| *20 juniper berries, crushed* |
| *2 tbsp. dry sherry* |
| *freshly ground black pepper* |
| *2 egg whites* |
| *⅔ cup buttermilk* |
| *1 tsp. grainy mustard* |
| *cucumber slices and parsley sprigs for garnish (optional)* |

Blanch the spinach in a large saucepan of boiling water for 10 seconds only. Drain the leaves, rinse them under cold running water, and dry them carefully with a clean dishtowel. Use enough spinach leaves to line the bottom and sides of a 1-quart terrine or loaf pan, letting them overhang the sides. Put the remaining leaves into a food processor together with the nutmeg and half of the salt, and chop them finely. Transfer the spinach to a bowl and set it aside to cool.

Preheat the oven to 350° F. Finely chop the veal in the food processor, add the cream cheese, heavy cream, whole egg, crushed juniper berries, sherry, some freshly ground black pepper, and the remaining salt, and process until all the ingredients are evenly mixed. Transfer the mixture to a bowl.

Beat the egg whites until they are stiff, then fold them into the veal. Spoon half of the mixture into the terrine or loaf pan and smooth the surface. Spoon the chopped spinach on top, cover with the remaining veal, and again smooth the surface. Cover with the overhanging spinach leaves, then with foil. Set the terrine in a roasting pan, pour in enough boiling water to come halfway up the sides of the terrine, and cook it in the oven for one hour.

Meanwhile, whisk the buttermilk and mustard together in a bowl. Remove the terrine from the water, take off the foil, pour off any excess liquid, and let it stand for five minutes. Run a knife around the edge of the terrine and turn it out onto a board. Cut it into neat slices and arrange them on individual plates. Pour some of the buttermilk sauce over each portion, and garnish each serving with cucumber slices and parsley sprigs, if desired.

EDITOR'S NOTE: *This dish can also be served cold—in which case let it cool in the terrine before turning it out.*

# Fricadelles with Cucumber Sauce

THESE DILL-FLAVORED MEAT PATTIES ARE A VERSION OF DANISH *FRIKADELLER*, WHICH ARE TRADITIONALLY TORPEDO-SHAPED.

Serves 6
Working (and total) time: about 1 hour

Calories **165**
Protein **16g.**
Cholesterol **70mg.**
Total fat **6g.**
Saturated fat **2g.**
Sodium **205mg.**

| |
|---|
| 1¼ lb. veal top round, trimmed of fat and diced |
| 2 slices whole-wheat bread, crusts removed |
| 1 onion, grated |
| 3 tbsp. sparkling mineral water |
| 2 egg whites |
| 1 tsp. chopped fresh dill |
| ½ tsp. ground allspice |
| ⅛ tsp. salt |
| freshly ground black pepper |
| 1 tbsp. virgin olive oil |

### Cucumber sauce

| |
|---|
| 1 large cucumber, peeled and finely diced |
| ⅔ cup unsalted chicken stock or unsalted veal stock (recipes, page 138) |
| ¼ cup sour cream |
| 2 tsp. cornstarch |
| 1½ tsp. chopped fresh dill |
| ground white pepper |
| ⅛ tsp. salt |

Put the veal into a food processor with the bread, onion, mineral water, egg whites, dill, allspice, salt, and some pepper, and chop finely. Transfer the mixture to a bowl. Dip two soupspoons into hot water and use them to form the chopped mixture into about 30 torpedo shapes, dipping the spoons back in the hot water after forming each one.

Heat the oil in a large, nonstick sauté pan or skillet over medium heat. Add the fricadelles and cook them until they are browned on all sides—about 10 minutes—turning once. Transfer the patties to a warmed dish, cover, and keep hot while preparing the sauce.

To make the sauce, add the cucumber to the pan and stir-fry for one minute. Pour in the stock, bring to a boil, and simmer for two to three minutes. Mix the sour cream and cornstarch together, add a few spoonfuls of the hot stock, then add this mixture to the pan and whisk over low heat for two minutes. Add the dill, some white pepper, and the salt. Serve hot, passing the sauce separately.

SUGGESTED ACCOMPANIMENT: *beet and lettuce salad.*

# Veal and Pasta Loaf with Tomato-Basil Ketchup

Serves 12 as a first course
Working time: about 1 hour and 10 minutes
Total time: about 2 hours and 20 minutes

Calories **143**
Protein **6g.**
Cholesterol **55mg.**
Total fat **3g.**
Saturated fat **1g.**
Sodium **115mg.**

| |
|---|
| 1 lb. veal top round or rump, trimmed of fat and ground or chopped (technique, page 15) |
| 1 tsp. virgin olive oil |
| 1 onion, chopped |
| 1 small garlic clove, crushed |
| 1 small zucchini, trimmed and grated |
| 2 small carrots, grated |
| 2 small parsnips, grated |
| ½ tsp. salt |
| freshly ground black pepper |
| 1 egg |
| 1 egg white |
| ½ lb. rigatoni or other small pasta shapes |
| 1 tbsp. cornstarch |
| ⅔ cup low-fat milk |
| ¼ tsp. freshly grated or ground nutmeg |
| 1 tbsp. freshly grated Parmesan cheese |
| curly endive for garnish (optional) |

**Tomato-basil ketchup**

| |
|---|
| 1½ lb. ripe tomatoes (4 medium), peeled, seeded, and chopped, or two 14 oz. cans tomatoes, chopped |
| 1 tsp. tomato paste |
| ½ tsp. sugar |
| 6 fresh basil leaves, shredded |

Heat the oil in a small, nonstick skillet over medium heat. Add the onion, garlic, and 2 tablespoons of water, and cook for about five minutes or until softened, stirring occasionally. Turn the onion and garlic into a mixing bowl, and add the veal, zucchini, carrots, parsnips, ¼ teaspoon of the salt, and some pepper.

Lightly beat the egg and egg white together in a small bowl. Add half of the egg to the veal mixture and work together thoroughly with your hands. Set aside. Cook the rigatoni in 3 quarts of boiling water with 1½ teaspoons of salt. Start testing the pasta after eight minutes, and cook it until it is al dente.

Meanwhile, make the white sauce. Mix the cornstarch with a little of the milk in a small cup. Put the remaining milk into a small saucepan and bring it to a boil, then lower the heat. Add the cornstarch mixture, stirring vigorously, and simmer gently for three minutes, stirring constantly. Remove the sauce from the heat and cool it slightly, then stir in the remaining egg mixture, the remaining ¼ teaspoon of salt, and the nutmeg. Drain the pasta, put it back into the pan, and mix it with the white sauce.

Preheat the oven to 325° F. Line the bottom of a loaf pan with a piece of dampened wax paper. Make a layer of just under one-third of the meat mixture on the bottom of the pan, pressing and spreading it out evenly. Cover with half of the pasta, then make another layer of the meat mixture. Top with the remaining pasta, and finish with the rest of the meat mixture.

(When laying the meat mixture over the pasta, press the mixture between your hands first, cover a small area at a time, and smooth the layer with the back of a spoon.) Sprinkle the top of the layered loaf with the Parmesan cheese. Place the loaf pan in a roasting pan and pour in enough boiling water to come at least 1 inch up the sides of the pan. Bake for one hour.

Meanwhile, make the tomato-basil ketchup. Put the tomatoes into a small, heavy-bottomed saucepan, adding a little water if you are using fresh tomatoes,

and simmer them until they are well reduced—about 10 minutes—stirring them from time to time. Sieve the tomatoes, and mix in the tomato paste and sugar. Allow them to cool.

When the loaf is ready, remove it from its water bath and let it cool in the pan for 10 minutes before turning it out. Remove the lining paper, then invert the loaf onto a cutting board. Cut it into thick slices. Stir the basil into the ketchup and serve it with the loaf. Garnish each portion with some curly endive, if desired.

# Veal and Mushroom Burgers with Mango-Pineapple Relish

Serves 4
Working time: about 50 minutes
Total time: about 1 hour and 35 minutes

Calories **325**
Protein **22g.**
Cholesterol **70mg.**
Total fat **9g.**
Saturated fat **3g.**
Sodium **370mg.**

| |
| --- |
| ¾ lb. veal top round or rump, trimmed of fat and finely chopped (technique, page 15) |
| 6 oz. mushrooms, wiped clean and finely chopped |
| 1 oz. walnuts (¼ cup), finely chopped |
| ½ tsp. salt |
| freshly ground black pepper |
| ⅛ to ¼ tsp. cayenne pepper |
| 1 egg white |
| 2 whole-wheat muffins, split in half |
| watercress or shredded lettuce |
| **Mango-pineapple relish** |
| 1 small unripe mango (about ½ lb.), peeled, pitted, and finely diced |
| ½ lb. fresh pineapple, finely diced |
| 1 small onion, finely chopped |
| 1½ tsp. freshly grated ginger |
| 1 small cinnamon stick |
| 4 whole cloves |
| 1 bay leaf |
| 1 lime, grated zest and juice |
| ½ tsp. Chinese chili sauce |

To make the relish, put the diced mango and pineapple into a heavy-bottomed, nonreactive saucepan, and add the onion, ginger, cinnamon stick, cloves, bay leaf, and lime zest and juice. Cover and cook over low heat for about 45 minutes, stirring occasionally, until the fruit is very tender. Add a tablespoon of water from time to time to prevent the relish from sticking to the pan. When the fruit is cooked, remove and discard the cinnamon stick, cloves, and bay leaf. Stir in the chili sauce and allow the mixture to cool.

To make the burgers, put the veal, mushrooms, and walnuts into a bowl, add the salt, some black pepper,

and the cayenne pepper, and work the mixture with your hands, adding enough egg white to bind. Divide the mixture into four portions and shape each into a neat burger about ½ inch thick. Place the burgers on a plate, cover, and chill for 20 minutes.

Preheat the grill. Grill the burgers for six to eight minutes on each side, or until they are cooked through and golden brown, turning them over carefully to avoid breaking them. Just before the burgers have finished cooking, toast the muffins on both sides. Cover the muffin halves with watercress or shredded lettuce, and place a burger on top. Serve immediately with the relish.

SUGGESTED ACCOMPANIMENT: cabbage and carrot coleslaw.
EDITOR'S NOTE: Alternatively, the veal, mushrooms, and walnuts can be finely chopped in a food processor, but the mixture will have a much smoother texture.

*5* Green peppercorns, garlic, and parsley enliven a beef roast that was braised on a bed of mushrooms and onions in a microwave oven (recipe, opposite).

# Microwaving Beef and Veal

A microwave oven encourages invention—and never more so, perhaps, than in the case of beef and veal, for the meat may be prepared successfully in any number of ways in a fraction of the time it would take by conventional cooking methods. Sealed in an oven-cooking bag and microwaved on medium power, for example, a roast braises in its own juices. It might also be cut into strips for a dish that looks and tastes like a stir-fry with very little oil, or be stuffed with a vegetable filling and served sliced.

Particular success attends recipes based on ground meat. The veal meatballs on page 137 are served with sweet-pepper sauce, while a Latin-American *picadillo* (*page 128*) highlights ground beef combined with raisins and olives.

A few simple techniques help ensure perfect results. Cutting beef or veal into smaller pieces allows it to cook more evenly in the microwave oven, but roasts can also be cooked whole. To keep it from drying out, cover the roast with plastic wrap during cooking. (Note: In the microwave oven, always use wrap that is free of plasticizers so that potentially harmful substances do not leach out into the food.) Avoid salting the roast beforehand—this tends to toughen the meat and draw out natural salts and moisture.

For the sake of succulence, tender cuts of beef and veal—including cutlets and meatballs—should be microwaved on high (100 percent power). Less tender cuts should be tightly covered and then simmered in liquid on medium (50 percent power).

Because food continues to cook after it emerges from the microwave oven, achieving the desired degree of doneness involves allowing for "standing time." Remove a roast from the oven slightly before the meat looks cooked, then insert an instant-reading thermometer in the center and let the meat stand until it reaches the proper internal temperature. In general, the standing time equals one-third to one-half of the cooking time; where such a step is required, the recipe instructions specify how long.

Many of the recipes in this chapter use a browning dish. This dish, designed specifically for the microwave oven, has a coating that allows the meat to be seared and browned in much the same way as under a broiler or in a skillet. When using a microwave browning dish it is important to follow the manufacturer's instructions carefully, as overheating can cause damage.

## Beef Braised on Mushrooms with Green-Peppercorn Persillade

Serves 6
Working time: about 30 minutes
Total time: about 1 hour

Calories **200**
Protein **25g.**
Cholesterol **62mg.**
Total fat **7g.**
Saturated fat **2g.**
Sodium **140mg.**

| |
|---|
| one 1¾-lb. rump roast, trimmed of fat |
| 1 lb. mushrooms, wiped clean and thinly sliced |
| 1 onion, finely chopped |
| 1 tsp. safflower oil |
| 2 tsp. green peppercorns, rinsed |
| ½ cup fresh parsley leaves |
| 3 garlic cloves |
| ¼ tsp. salt |
| 2 tbsp. unbleached all-purpose flour |

Combine the mushrooms, onion, and oil in an 8-inch-square baking dish. Cover the dish with heavy-duty plastic wrap pulled back at one edge to prevent the buildup of steam, and microwave the vegetables on high for five minutes.

While the mushrooms are cooking, prepare the green-peppercorn *persillade*. Place the green peppercorns, parsley, and garlic on a cutting board, and sprinkle them with the salt; finely chop the mixture.

Pierce the roast in about 15 places with the tip of a small knife. Press some of the *persillade* into each of the incisions. Rub any remaining *persillade* on the outside of the roast.

When the mushrooms have finished cooking, stir the flour into them. Set the roast on top of the mushrooms and cover the dish as before. Cook the meat on medium (50 percent power) for 14 to 16 minutes for medium-rare meat. Let the roast stand, still covered, an additional 10 minutes before carving. (At this point, the internal temperature of the meat should have risen to 145° F.; if it has not, microwave the roast on high for two to three minutes more.)

Cut the roast into very thin slices; divide the meat and mushrooms among six warmed dinner plates. Serve immediately.

SUGGESTED ACCOMPANIMENT: *steamed potatoes and carrots.*

## Picadillo

THIS ADAPTATION OF A LATIN-AMERICAN FAVORITE
FEATURES RAISINS, OLIVES, AND CHICKPEAS IN ADDITION
TO THE CHOPPED MEAT.

Serves 6
Working time: about 45 minutes
Total time: about 3 hours (includes soaking)

Calories **225**
Protein **18g.**
Cholesterol **35mg.**
Total fat **6g.**
Saturated fat **1g.**
Sodium **235mg.**

| |
|---|
| 1 lb. beef round, trimmed of fat and ground or chopped (technique, page 15) |
| 1 cup dried chickpeas, picked over |
| 1 onion, chopped |
| 4 garlic cloves, finely chopped |
| 1 tsp. safflower oil |
| 28 oz. canned unsalted whole tomatoes, drained and crushed |
| ½ cup golden raisins |
| 12 pitted green olives, rinsed |
| ½ tsp. cinnamon |
| ½ tsp. ground allspice |
| ¼ tsp. cayenne pepper |
| 2 bay leaves |

Rinse the chickpeas under cold running water, then put them into a large, heavy-bottomed pot with enough water to cover them by about 3 inches. Cover the pot, leaving the lid ajar, and slowly bring the liquid to a boil over medium-low heat on the stovetop. Boil the chickpeas for two minutes, then turn off the heat and soak the chickpeas, covered, for at least one hour. Return the chickpeas to a boil, lower the heat, and simmer them until they are tender—about one hour.

Combine the onion, garlic, and oil in a large bowl. Cover the bowl with plastic wrap pulled back at one edge, and microwave the vegetables on high for four minutes. Add the beef and cook the mixture, uncovered, on medium (50 percent power) for five minutes. Stir the beef, breaking it into small pieces, and cook it on medium for three minutes more.

Drain the chickpeas and add them to the beef mixture. Stir in the tomatoes, raisins, olives, cinnamon, allspice, cayenne pepper, and bay leaves. Cook the *picadillo*, uncovered, on high for 15 minutes, stirring it every five minutes. Remove the bay leaves and let the *picadillo* stand for five minutes before serving.

SUGGESTED ACCOMPANIMENT: *rice with sweet red pepper.*

EDITOR'S NOTE: *Canned chickpeas can be used in this recipe, thus greatly reducing the cooking time, but the sodium content of the dish will be increased.*

# Meatballs in Caper Sauce

Serves 4 as an appetizer
Working time: about 20 minutes
Total time: about 30 minutes

Calories **120**
Protein **14g.**
Cholesterol **34mg.**
Total fat **4g.**
Saturated fat **1g.**
Sodium **190mg.**

| |
|---|
| 10 oz. beef round, trimmed of fat and ground or chopped (technique, page 15) |
| 1 small onion, chopped |
| 1 cup unsalted brown stock or unsalted chicken stock (recipes, page 138) |
| ¼ cup rolled oats |
| 1 tbsp. chopped fresh parsley, plus sprig for garnish |
| ¼ tsp. freshly grated or ground nutmeg |
| grated zest of 1 lemon |
| freshly ground black pepper |
| 1 tsp. cornstarch, mixed with 1 tbsp. water |
| 1 tbsp. plain low-fat yogurt |
| 1 tsp. sour cream |
| 1 tsp. capers, rinsed and chopped |

Place the onion in a 1-quart baking dish. Cover the dish with plastic wrap pulled back at one edge and microwave on high for three minutes. Put the onion into a bowl. Add the stock to the dish and cook it on high until it comes to a simmer—about four minutes.

While the stock is heating, add the beef, rolled oats, ½ tablespoon of the parsley, the nutmeg, the lemon zest, and a liberal grinding of pepper to the onion. Knead the mixture to mix it well, then form it into 16 meatballs. Drop the meatballs into the heated stock and cook them, covered, on high for four minutes.

Using a slotted spoon, transfer the meatballs to a serving dish. Discard all but ½ cup of the cooking liquid in the baking dish; stir the cornstarch mixture into the remaining liquid. Cook the mixture on high until it thickens—about 30 seconds. Let the thickened stock cool for one minute, then stir in the yogurt, sour cream, capers, and remaining ½ tablespoon of parsley. Pour the sauce over the meatballs and serve them while they are still hot, garnished with the parsley.

# Lime-Ginger Beef

Serves 4
Working time: about 25 minutes
Total time: about 45 minutes

| | |
|---|---|
| Calories **240**<br>Protein **25g.**<br>Cholesterol **65mg.**<br>Total fat **10g.**<br>Saturated fat **3g.**<br>Sodium **180mg.** | *2 top loin steaks (about 10 oz. each), trimmed*<br>*of fat and cut into thin strips* |
| | *freshly ground black pepper* |
| | *1 tbsp. safflower oil* |
| | *2 scallions, trimmed and sliced into thin strips* |
| | *1 large carrot, julienned* |
| | *1 sweet red pepper, seeded, deribbed,*<br>*and julienned* |
| | **Lime-ginger sauce** |
| | *grated zest and juice of 1 lime* |
| | *1 tsp. grated fresh ginger* |
| | *2 tbsp. dry sherry* |
| | *2 tsp. low-sodium soy sauce* |
| | *½ tsp. finely chopped garlic* |
| | *1 tbsp. sugar* |
| | *1 tbsp. cornstarch, mixed with ¼ cup water* |

Preheat a microwave browning dish on high for the maximum time allowed in the dish's instruction manual. While the dish is heating, combine all the ingredients for the lime-ginger sauce in a small bowl. Set the bowl aside. Season the beef strips with a generous grinding of black pepper.

When the browning dish is heated, brush ½ tablespoon of the safflower oil evenly over the dish to coat it. Sear half of the beef strips on the dish, stirring and turning the meat with a wooden spoon. Once the beef has been seared—after one or two minutes—transfer it to a baking dish. Wipe off the browning dish with a paper towel and reheat it for three minutes. Brush the remaining ½ tablespoon of oil onto the dish and sear the remaining beef in the same way. Add the beef to the baking dish.

Add the scallions, carrot, and red-pepper strips to the beef. Pour the sauce over all and microwave the mixture on high for three minutes. Serve the beef and vegetables from the baking dish or transfer them to a platter; serve at once.

SUGGESTED ACCOMPANIMENT: *steamed rice.*

# Veal Cutlets in Tarragon and Mushroom Sauce

Serves 4
Working time: about 15 minutes
Total time: about 1 hour and 15 minutes
(includes marinating)

Calories **240**
Protein **22g.**
Cholesterol **100mg.**
Total fat **11g.**
Saturated fat **3g.**
Sodium **215mg.**

| |
|---|
| 4 thin veal cutlets (about 4 oz. each) |
| 2 tbsp. virgin olive oil |
| 2 tbsp. finely shredded fresh tarragon leaves |
| freshly ground black pepper |
| **Mushroom sauce** |
| ¼ cup Marsala |
| 6 oz. mushrooms, trimmed and very thinly sliced |
| 2 tbsp. unbleached all-purpose flour |
| 2 tbsp. sour cream mixed with enough skim milk to make ⅔ cup |
| ¼ tsp. salt |

Blend the oil with 1 tablespoon of the tarragon and some pepper in a shallow dish. Add the cutlets and turn them in the oil until they are evenly coated. Cover the dish and let the veal marinate at room temperature for at least one hour.

Heat a browning dish on high for the maximum time allowed in the instruction manual. Brown the cutlets on each side in the hot dish, then cover the dish with plastic wrap pulled back at one edge and microwave on high for one and a half minutes. Transfer the cutlets to a plate, cover them, and set them aside.

To make the sauce, stir the Marsala into the browning dish, add the mushrooms, and microwave on high for two minutes. Blend the flour with the sour-cream mixture, the remaining tarragon, the salt, and a little black pepper until smooth. Stir into the mushrooms and microwave on high for one minute. Return the veal to the dish, coat well with the sauce, and microwave for two and a half to three minutes, repositioning the cutlets halfway through cooking. Serve at once.

SUGGESTED ACCOMPANIMENTS: *rice with peas, scallions, and sweet peppers; French bread.*

# Microwave Stir-Fry

Serves 4
Working (and total) time: about 25 minutes

Calories **260**
Protein **24g.**
Cholesterol **90mg.**
Total fat **14g.**
Saturated fat **3g.**
Sodium **140mg.**

| |
|---|
| 1 lb. thin veal cutlets, cut into very thin strips |
| ½ lb. broccoli, trimmed and cut into small florets (about 3 cups) |
| 2 tbsp. virgin olive oil |
| 3 tbsp. hoisin sauce |
| 1 small sweet red pepper, cut into thin julienne |
| 8 radishes, thinly sliced |
| 1 garlic clove, crushed |
| 6 oz. fresh pineapple, cut into small pieces (about 1 cup) |
| 1 oz. unsalted cashew nuts (¼ cup) |

Put the broccoli into a dish with 2 tablespoons of water, cover the dish with plastic wrap pulled back at one edge, and microwave on high for one and a half minutes. Pour the broccoli into a colander and rinse under cold water to refresh. Drain well and set aside.

Heat a browning dish on high for the maximum time allowed in the instruction manual. Brush 1 tablespoon of the oil over the dish to coat it evenly, and add the veal strips. Microwave on high for one and a half minutes, stirring once. Remove the veal from the dish and set it aside.

In a small bowl, mix 1 tablespoon of the meat juices from the browning dish with the hoisin sauce; discard the rest of the meat juices. Coat the browning dish with the remaining oil, and microwave the oil on high for 30 seconds. Add the julienned red pepper, sliced radishes, and crushed garlic, and microwave on high for one minute.

Stir in the pineapple, cashew nuts, and broccoli florets, then microwave on high for one minute. Add the veal and hoisin sauce, stir well, and microwave on high for two and a half to three minutes, stirring halfway through cooking. Serve immediately.

SUGGESTED ACCOMPANIMENT: *steamed rice.*

## Zucchini-Stuffed Veal Roast

Serves 4
Working time: about 40 minutes
Total time: about 1 hour and 50 minutes
(includes marinating)

| | |
|---|---|
| Calories **240** | 1 lb. veal rump in one piece, trimmed of fat |
| Protein **22g.** | 1 tbsp. virgin olive oil |
| Cholesterol **90mg.** | 1 garlic clove, crushed |
| Total fat **13g.** | 1 tsp. paprika |
| Saturated fat **3g.** | 2 tbsp. brandy |
| Sodium **210mg.** | **Zucchini stuffing** |
| | 1 tbsp. virgin olive oil |
| | 1 small onion, very finely chopped |
| | ¾ lb. zucchini (2 small), coarsely grated |
| | 1 tbsp. chopped fresh marjoram, or 1 tsp. dried marjoram |
| | ¼ tsp. salt |
| | freshly ground black pepper |
| | ¼ cup black olives, pitted and finely chopped |

Slice the veal horizontally almost in two *(opposite, Step 1)*. Open it out and place it between two sheets of plastic wrap, flatten it with a meat bat or rolling pin as described in Step 1 on page 32, and refrigerate it.

To make the stuffing, place the oil in a shallow dish,

add the onion, and microwave it on high for two minutes until it is softened. Stir in the zucchini, cover with plastic wrap pulled back at one edge, and microwave on high for seven to eight minutes until they are softened, stirring every two minutes. Remove from the oven, and stir in the marjoram, salt, some pepper, and the olives. Allow the mixture to cool.

Spread the stuffing evenly over one half of the flattened veal, then fold the other half over to enclose the stuffing and tie securely *(opposite, Steps 2 and 3)*.

Blend the olive oil, garlic, and paprika together in a shallow dish, add the veal, and turn it gently in this marinade until it is evenly coated. Cover the veal and marinate it at room temperature for one hour.

Heat a browning dish on high for the maximum time allowed in the instruction manual. Transfer the veal to the browning dish and brown on both sides. Cover as before and microwave on high for five minutes, turning it over after two and a half minutes. Transfer the veal to a serving plate, cover with foil and allow to stand for two minutes, then carefully remove the string. Meanwhile, stir the brandy into the dish, microwave on high for two minutes, and strain over the veal. Serve the veal hot or cold, cut into thin slices.

SUGGESTED ACCOMPANIMENT: *snow peas.*

## Stuffing and Tying a Veal Roast

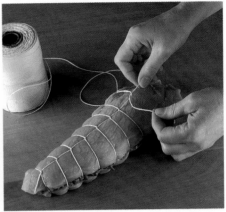

**1** *MAKING A POCKET. With a sharp knife, slice the veal (here, a piece of rump) horizontally almost in two. Lay the veal on a sheet of plastic wrap. Open out the meat and cover it with a second piece of wrap.*

**2** *SPREADING THE STUFFING. Using a meat bat or rolling pin, gently pound the meat until it spreads enough to accommodate a stuffing. Spoon the stuffing (recipe, opposite) evenly over one half of the flattened veal. Fold the other half of the veal over to enclose the stuffing.*

**3** *SECURING THE STUFFING. Loop the free end of a ball of string around one end of the rump and tie a knot. Without cutting the string, make successive loops at 1¼-inch intervals along the rump; tighten each loop by pulling the string as you go. Secure the parcel by bringing the string under the entire length of the roast and knotting it to the free end.*

# Medallions of Veal with Green Peppercorns and Tomato Sauce

Serves 6
Working time: about 20 minutes
Total time: about 1 hour and 20 minutes
(includes marinating)

| | |
|---|---|
| Calories **150** | 6 medallions of veal (about 4 oz. each), trimmed of fat and neatly tied |
| Protein **22g.** | |
| Cholesterol **90mg.** | 1 tbsp. virgin olive oil |
| Total fat **6g.** | 1 tsp. dried green peppercorns, crushed |
| Saturated fat **2g.** | 2 tbsp. brandy |
| Sodium **180mg.** | ¾ lb. ripe tomatoes, peeled, seeded, and chopped |
| | 2 tsp. mixed dried herbs |
| | 1 garlic clove, crushed |
| | ¼ tsp. salt |
| | freshly ground black pepper |
| | watercress for garnish |

Mix the oil with the peppercorns in a shallow dish, add the medallions of veal, and turn them in the oil until they are evenly coated. Cover and allow to marinate at room temperature for at least one hour.

Heat a browning dish on high for the maximum time allowed in the instruction manual. Brown the medallions on both sides in the hot dish; cover with plastic wrap pulled back at one edge and microwave on high for three minutes, turning them over after one and a half minutes. Transfer the meat to a serving dish, cover with foil, and set aside. Stir the brandy into the browning dish and microwave on high for one minute, or until it is reduced by half. Add the tomatoes, herbs, garlic, salt, and pepper. Cover as before and microwave on high for four minutes, stirring frequently. Pour into a gravy boat. Meanwhile, microwave the medallions on high for one minute more. Garnish with watercress and serve immediately with the sauce.

SUGGESTED ACCOMPANIMENT: *celery or fennel hearts.*

# Medallions of Veal and Vegetables in Yogurt-Lemon Sauce

Serves 6
Working time: about 30 minutes
Total time: about 1 hour (includes marinating)

Calories **190**
Protein **24g.**
Cholesterol **90mg.**
Total fat **8g.**
Saturated fat **2g.**
Sodium **190mg.**

| |
|---|
| 6 medallions of veal (about 4 oz. each), trimmed of fat and neatly tied |
| 2 tbsp. virgin olive oil |
| 1 garlic clove, crushed |
| freshly ground black pepper |
| 2 small onions, quartered |
| 4 asparagus spears, trimmed and thinly sliced diagonally |
| ¼ lb. mushrooms, wiped clean and stems trimmed |
| ¼ lb. frozen peas |
| 2 tbsp. unbleached all-purpose flour |
| 1 lemon, finely grated zest only |
| ¼ tsp. salt |
| 3 tbsp. plain low-fat yogurt |
| lemon wedges and parsley sprigs for garnish (optional) |

In a shallow dish, mix 1 tablespoon of the olive oil with the crushed garlic and some black pepper. Add the medallions and turn them in the oil until they are evenly coated. Cover them and marinate them at room temperature for at least 30 minutes.

About 15 minutes before cooking the medallions, put the remaining oil into a shallow dish and microwave it on high for 30 seconds. Add the onions and asparagus, cover with plastic wrap pulled back at one edge, and microwave on high for four minutes, stirring after two minutes. Add the mushrooms and peas, cover, and microwave on high for three minutes, stirring after one and a half minutes. Meanwhile, in a small bowl, blend the flour with the lemon zest, salt, some pepper, and the yogurt until the mixture is smooth. Stir into the vegetables and microwave the mixture on high for three minutes, stirring after each minute. Remove the vegetables from the oven and keep them warm while cooking the medallions.

Heat a browning dish on high for the maximum time allowed in the instruction manual. Brown both sides of the medallions in the hot dish. Cover with plastic wrap pulled back at one edge and microwave on high for one and a half minutes, then turn the medallions over and microwave for one minute more. Remove the meat to a hot serving dish, cover it with foil, and allow it to stand for one minute.

Meanwhile, microwave the cooked vegetables on high for one minute to heat them through. Serve the medallions accompanied by the vegetables and garnished, if desired, with the lemon wedges and parsley.

## Meatballs with Sweet-Pepper Sauce

Serves 4
Working (and total) time: about 1 hour

Calories **280**
Protein **26g.**
Cholesterol **90mg.**
Total fat **12g.**
Saturated fat **4g.**
Sodium **385mg.**

| |
|---|
| 1 lb. veal rump or top round, trimmed of fat and very finely ground or chopped (technique, page 15) |
| ¾ cup fresh whole-wheat breadcrumbs |
| 1 small onion, finely chopped |
| 2 tbsp. chopped fresh parsley |
| 1 tsp. mixed dried herbs |
| 2 tbsp. virgin olive oil |
| 1 egg white |
| freshly ground black pepper |
| **Sweet-pepper sauce** |
| 1 onion, thinly sliced |
| 1 small sweet red pepper, thinly sliced |
| 1 small sweet green pepper, thinly sliced |
| 3 celery stalks, thinly sliced |
| 2 tsp. paprika |
| 2 tsp. tomato paste |
| 1¼ cups unsalted veal stock or unsalted chicken stock (recipes, page 138) |
| ¼ tsp. salt |

Place the veal in a large bowl with the breadcrumbs, onion, parsley, mixed dried herbs, 1 tablespoon of the oil, and the egg white. Season with pepper, then mix the ingredients thoroughly until they are smooth. Divide the mixture into 20 equal portions. With wet hands, roll each portion into a neat ball.

Heat a browning dish on high for the maximum time allowed in the instruction manual. Add the remaining oil to the dish. Place the meatballs in the dish and microwave them on high, uncovered, for five to six minutes, turning and repositioning them every two minutes. Transfer them to a plate and set them aside.

To make the sauce, add the sliced onion, red and green peppers, and celery to the oil remaining in the browning dish, and stir. Microwave on high, uncovered, for four to five minutes, until the vegetables are softened. Stir in the paprika and microwave for 30 seconds. Stir in the tomato paste, stock, and salt. Cover the dish with plastic wrap pulled back at one edge and microwave on high for eight minutes, stirring every two minutes.

Return the meatballs to the dish, coat them well with the sauce, then microwave on high for two minutes. Serve immediately.

SUGGESTED ACCOMPANIMENTS: *noodles; green salad.*

Making your own stock is easy, and the recipes that follow tell you how. Canned chicken stock may be substituted, but look for the low-sodium kind; if you cannot get it, eliminate the salt from the recipe you are preparing. Canned beef stock is very salty and does not have the quality of brown stock; again, if you must use it, be sure to leave out the salt in the recipe.

## Chicken Stock

Makes about 2 quarts
Working time: about 20 minutes
Total time: about 3 hours

| |
|---|
| 5 lb. uncooked chicken trimmings and bones, the bones cracked with a heavy knife |
| 2 carrots, scrubbed, cut into ½-inch-thick rounds |
| 2 celery stalks, cut into 1-inch pieces |
| 2 large onions (about 1 lb.), cut in half, one half stuck with 2 cloves |
| 2 sprigs fresh thyme, or ½ tsp. dried thyme leaves |
| 1 or 2 bay leaves |
| 10 to 15 parsley stems |
| 5 black peppercorns |

Put the chicken trimmings and bones into a heavy stockpot; pour in enough water to cover them by about 2 inches. Bring the liquid to a boil over medium heat, skimming off the scum that rises to the surface. Lower the heat and simmer the liquid for 10 minutes, skimming and adding a little cold water to help precipitate the scum.

Add the vegetables, herbs, and peppercorns, and submerge them in the liquid. If necessary, pour in enough additional water to cover the contents of the pot. Simmer the stock for two to three hours, skimming as necessary to remove the scum.

Strain the stock and discard the solids. Allow the stock to stand until it is tepid, then refrigerate it overnight to allow the fat to congeal. Spoon off and discard the layer of fat.

Tightly covered and refrigerated, the stock may be safely kept for two or three days. Stored in small, tightly covered freezer containers and frozen, the stock may be kept for as long as six months.

EDITOR'S NOTE: *The chicken gizzard and heart may be added to the stock. Wings and necks—rich in natural gelatin—produce a particularly gelatinous stock, ideal for sauces and jellied dishes. The liver should never be used.*

## Brown Stock

Makes about 3 quarts
Working time: about 40 minutes
Total time: about 5 hours and 30 minutes

| |
|---|
| 3 lb. veal breast (or veal-shank or beef-shank meat), cut into 3-inch pieces |
| 3 lb. uncooked veal or beef bones, cracked |
| 2 onions, quartered |
| 2 celery stalks, chopped |
| 2 carrots, sliced |
| 3 unpeeled garlic cloves, crushed |
| 8 black peppercorns |
| 3 whole cloves |
| 2 tsp. chopped fresh thyme, or ½ tsp. dried thyme leaves |
| 1 bay leaf |

Preheat the oven to 425° F. Place the meat, bones, onions, celery, and carrots in a roasting pan, and bake them until they are brown—about one hour. Transfer them to a stockpot. Pour 2 cups of water into the roasting pan and scrape up the browned bits from the bottom of the pan. Pour the liquid into the pot.

Add the garlic, peppercorns, and cloves. Pour in enough water to cover the contents of the pot by about 3 inches. Bring to a boil, then lower the heat to a simmer, and skim any impurities from the surface. Add the thyme and bay leaf, then simmer over low heat for four hours, skimming occasionally. Strain the stock and discard the solids. Allow the stock to stand until it is tepid, then refrigerate it overnight. Spoon off and discard the layer of congealed fat.

Tightly covered and refrigerated, the stock may be safely kept for two or three days. Stored in small, tightly covered freezer containers and frozen, the stock may be kept for as long as six months.

EDITOR'S NOTE: *Browning in the oven should produce a stock with a rich, mahogany color. If the stock does not seem dark enough, cook 1 tablespoon of tomato paste in a small pan over medium heat, stirring constantly, until it darkens—about three minutes. Add this to the stock about one hour before the end of the cooking time. Any combination of meat and bones may be used. Ask your butcher to crack the bones.*

## Veal Stock

For a light veal stock, follow the chicken stock recipe, but substitute 5 pounds of cracked veal bones for the chicken bones.

# Glossary

**Arrowroot:** a tasteless, starchy, white powder, refined from the root of a tropical plant, that is used as a thickener. Unlike flour, it is transparent when cooked.

**Arugula** (also called rocket, rocket cress, *roquette, ruchetta,* and *rugula*): a peppery-flavored salad plant with long, leafy stems, popular in Italy.

**Balsamic vinegar:** a mildly acid, intensely fragrant wine-based vinegar made in northern Italy. Traditionally it is aged in wooden casks.

**Bâtonnet** (also called bâton): a piece of vegetable that has been cut in the shape of a stick—usually about 1½ inches long and ¼ inch square.

**Belgian endive:** a small, cigar-shaped vegetable composed of many tightly wrapped white to pale yellow leaves that have a pleasant bitter flavor.

**Bulgur:** whole-wheat kernels that have been steamed, dried, and cracked.

**Butterfly:** to split a boneless cut of meat in half horizontally, leaving the halves hinged on one side.

**Buttermilk:** a tangy, cultured-milk product that, despite its name, contains about one-third less fat than whole milk.

**Calorie** (or kilocalorie): a precise measure of the energy a food supplies when it is broken down for use in the body.

**Capers:** the pickled flower buds of the caper plant, a shrub native to the Mediterranean. Capers should be rinsed before use to rid them of excess salt.

**Caramelize:** to heat sugar, or a naturally sugar-rich food such as onion, until the sugar becomes brown and syrupy.

**Cardamom:** the bittersweet, aromatic dried seeds or whole pods of a plant in the ginger family. Cardamom seeds may be used whole or ground.

**Cayenne pepper:** a fiery powder ground from the seeds and pods of various red chili peppers, used in small amounts to heighten other flavors.

**Celeriac** (also called celery root): the knobby, tuberous root of a plant in the celery family.

**Ceps** (also called porcini): wild mushrooms with a pungent, earthy flavor that survives drying or long cooking; they are often used in French and Italian cooking. Dried ceps should be soaked in hot water before use.

**Channel knife:** a kitchen utensil used to create small grooves in vegetables for decorative purposes.

**Chanterelle** (also called girolle): a variety of wild mushroom that is trumpet shaped and yellow-orange in color. Chanterelles are available fresh or dried; dried chanterelles should be soaked in hot water before use.

**Chiffonade:** a leafy vegetable sliced into shreds.

**Chili paste:** a robust, spicy paste made of chili peppers, salt, and other ingredients, among them garlic and black beans. Numerous kinds are available in Asian markets.

**Chili peppers** (also called chilies): a variety of hot red or green peppers. *Serranos* and jalapeños are small, fresh green chilies that are extremely hot. *Anchos* are dried *poblano* chilies that are mildly hot and dark red in color. Fresh or dried, chili peppers contain volatile oils that can irritate the skin and eyes; they must be handled with extreme care *(cautionary note, page 8)*. See also Chili paste.

**Chinese chili sauce:** a condiment available in Asian markets and many supermarkets.

**Chinese dried mushrooms:** available in Asian markets and many supermarkets. They should be soaked in hot water before use.

**Chinese five-spice powder** (also called five heavenly spices and five fragrant spices): a pungent blend of ground spices, most often fennel seeds, star anise, cloves, cinnamon or cassia, and Sichuan peppercorns; it should be used sparingly. If five-spice powder is unavailable, substitute a mixture of equal parts ground Sichuan peppercorns, cloves, cinnamon, and fennel seeds.

**Cholesterol:** a waxlike substance that is manufactured in the human body and also found in foods of animal origin. Although a certain amount of cholesterol is necessary for proper body functioning, an excess can accumulate in the arteries, contributing to heart disease. See also Monounsaturated fats; Polyunsaturated fats; Saturated fats.

**Cilantro** (also called fresh coriander and Chinese parsley): the leaves of the coriander plant.

**Clarified butter:** a clear cooking fat made by melting butter slowly on the top of the stove so that the milk solids sink to the bottom of the pan, leaving a clear residue. Clarified butter is useful for sautéing over high heat because it does not burn easily.

**Coriander** (also called coriander seed): the dried fruit of the coriander plant.

**Cornichons:** small, French, sour gherkin pickles.

**Cornstarch:** a starchy white powder made from corn kernels and used to thicken sauces. Like arrowroot, it is transparent when cooked and makes a more efficient thickener than flour. When cooked by conventional methods, a liquid containing cornstarch must be stirred constantly in the early stages to prevent lumps from forming.

**Crystallized ginger** (also called candied ginger): stems of young ginger preserved with sugar. Crystallized ginger should not be confused with ginger in syrup.

**Cumin:** the seeds of an umbelliferous plant similar to fennel used, whole or powdered, as a spice, especially in Indian and Latin-American dishes.

**Daikon radish:** a long, white Japanese radish.

**Dark sesame oil:** a seasoning oil, high in polyunsaturated fats, that is made from toasted sesame seeds. Because dark sesame oil has a relatively low smoking point, it is rarely used for sautéing. Dark sesame oil should not be confused or replaced with lighter sesame cooking oils.

**Deglaze:** to dissolve the browned bits left in a pan after roasting or sautéing by stirring in wine, stock, water, or cream.

**Dijon mustard:** a smooth or grainy mustard once manufactured only in Dijon, France; may be flavored with herbs, green peppercorns, or white wine.

**Fennel** (also called anise, finochio, and Florence fennel): a vegetable with feathery green tops and a thick, bulbous stalk. It has a milky, licorice flavor and can be eaten raw or cooked.

**Fennel seeds:** the aromatic dried seeds of the herb fennel, a relative of the vegetable fennel; they are used as a licorice-flavored seasoning in many Italian dishes.

**Flute:** to make a series of small, decorative furrows in a vegetable, fruit, piecrust, etc.

**Ghee:** clarified butter, used especially in Indian cooking, made from the milk of cows or water buffaloes. See also Clarified butter.

**Ginger:** the spicy, buff-colored, rootlike stem of the ginger plant, used as a seasoning either fresh, or dried and powdered. Dried ginger makes a poor substitute for fresh ginger. See also Crystallized ginger.

**Grape leaves:** the tender, delicately flavored leaves of the grapevine. Grape leaves are used in many Mediterranean cuisines as wrappers for savory fillings. Fresh grape leaves should be cooked for five minutes in boiling water before they are used in a recipe; grape leaves packed in brine should be thoroughly rinsed before use.

**Hoisin sauce:** a thick, dark, reddish brown sauce generally made from soybeans, flour, garlic, sugar, and spices.

**Julienne:** to slice food into matchstick-size pieces; also the name for the pieces themselves.

**Juniper berries:** the dried berries of the juniper tree, used as a key flavoring in gin as well as in meat marinades.

**Madeira:** a fortified wine from the island of Madeira. It has an underlying burned flavor, which is the result of heating the wine after fermentation.

**Mango:** a fruit grown throughout the tropics, with sweet, succulent, yellow-orange flesh that is extremely rich in vitamin A. Like papaya, it may cause an allergic reaction in some individuals.

**Marbling:** the intramuscular fat that is found within meat. This fat cannot be trimmed away, but much of it can be rendered during cooking.

**Marinade:** a mixture of aromatic ingredients in which meat is allowed to stand before cooking to enrich its flavor. Some marinades will tenderize meat, but they do not penetrate deeply.

**Marsala:** a fortified dessert wine named after the region of Sicily where it originated. Most varieties are sweet in flavor and brown in color.

**Meat thermometer:** a thermometer that registers the internal temperature of a roast or steak.

**Mirin:** a sweet Japanese cooking wine that is made from rice. If mirin is unavailable, substitute white wine or sake mixed with a little sugar.

**Mixed dried herbs** (also called fines herbes): a standard, commercially prepared mixture of dried herbs, used for flavoring sauces, soups, omelets, etc., or as a garnish.

**Monounsaturated fats:** one of the three types of fats found in foods. Monounsaturated fats are believed not to raise the level of cholesterol in the blood.

**Nan bread:** a flat, leavened Afghan bread. Available in Middle Eastern groceries and some supermarkets.

**Nappa cabbage** (also called Chinese cabbage): an elongated cabbage resembling romaine lettuce, with long, broad ribs and crinkled, light green to white leaves.

**Olive oil:** any of various grades of oil extracted from olives. Extra virgin olive oil has a full, fruity flavor and very low acidity. Virgin olive oil is lighter in flavor and slightly higher in acidity. Pure olive oil, a blend of olive oils, has the lightest taste and the highest acidity. To prevent rancidity, the oil should be stored in a cool, dark place.

**Papaya:** a tropical fruit, rich in vitamins A and C, whose juice contains the enzyme papain; the action of this enzyme breaks down the protein in meat and tenderizes it. Like mango, papaya may cause an allergic reaction in some individuals.

**Persillade:** a French term for chopped parsley mixed with garlic.

**Phyllo** (also spelled "filo"): a paper-thin flour-and-water pastry popular in Greece and the Middle East. It can be made at home or bought, fresh or frozen, from delicatessens and stores specializing in Middle Eastern food. Because frozen phyllo dries out easily, it should be thawed in the refrigerator, and any phyllo sheets not in use should be covered with a damp towel.

**Pine nuts:** seeds from the cone of the stone pine, a tree native to the Mediterranean. The buttery flavor of pine nuts can be heightened by light toasting.

**Polyunsaturated fats:** one of the three types of fat found in foods. They exist in abundance in such vegetable oils as safflower, sunflower, corn, or soybean. Polyunsaturated fats lower the level of cholesterol in the blood.

**Port:** a sweet fortified wine originally produced in northern Portugal and shipped through the city of Oporto.

**Pot roast:** a chunky piece of beef cooked by braising.

**Prosciutto:** a dry-cured Italian ham that is sliced paper-thin before serving. The best is produced near Parma, Italy.

**Recommended Dietary Allowance (RDA):** the average daily amount of an essential nutrient as determined for groups of healthy people of various ages by the National Research Council.

**Reduce:** to boil down a liquid or sauce to concentrate its flavor or thicken its consistency.

**Rice vinegar:** a mild, fragrant vinegar that is less assertive than cider vinegar or distilled white vinegar. It is available in dark, light, seasoned, and sweetened varieties; Japanese rice vinegar generally is milder than the Chinese version.

**Safflower oil:** the vegetable oil that contains the highest proportion of polyunsaturated fats.

**Saffron:** the dried, yellowish red stigmas, or threads, of the saffron crocus (*Crocus sativus*); saffron yields a pungent flavor and a brilliant yellow color. Powdered saffron may be substituted for the threads but has less flavor.

**Saturated fats:** one of the three types of fats found in food. Existing in abundance in animal products and in coconut and palm oils, they raise the level of cholesterol in the blood. Because high blood-cholesterol levels may cause heart disease, consumption of saturated fat should be restricted to less than 15 percent of the calories provided by the daily diet.

**Scaloppine:** cutlets sliced or pounded thin.

**Sear:** to brown the surface of meat by a short application of intense heat. Searing adds flavor as well as color.

**Sesame oil:** see Dark sesame oil.

**Shallot:** a mild variety of onion, with a subtle flavor and papery, red-brown skin. If shallots are unavailable, substitute scallions.

**Shiitake mushrooms:** a variety of mushroom, originally cultivated only in Japan, that is sold fresh or dried. The dried version should be stored in a cool, dry place; it may be reconstituted by 20 to 30 minutes' soaking in water before use.

**Sodium:** a nutrient essential to maintaining the proper balance of fluids in the body. In most diets, a major source of the element is table salt, which contains 40 percent sodium. Excess sodium may contribute to high blood pressure, which increases the risk of heart disease. One teaspoon of salt, with 2,132 milligrams of sodium, contains about two-thirds of the maximum "safe and adequate" daily intake recommended by the National Research Council.

**Soy sauce:** a savory, salty brown liquid made from fermented soybeans. One tablespoon of ordinary soy sauce contains about 1,030 milligrams of sodium; lower-sodium variations, as used in the recipes in this book, may contain as little as half that amount.

**Stir-fry:** to cook thin pieces of meat or vegetables, or a combination of both, over high heat in a small amount of oil, stirring constantly to ensure even cooking in a short time. The traditional cooking vessel is a Chinese wok; a heavy-bottomed skillet may also be used.

**Stock:** a savory broth that is made by simmering aromatic vegetables, herbs, spices, bones, and meat trimmings in water. Stock is often used as a flavor-rich liquid for braising meat and making sauces.

**Sun-dried tomatoes:** tomatoes that have been naturally dried in the sun to concentrate their flavor and preserve them; some are then packed in oil with seasoning and herbs.

**Sweet chili sauce:** any of a group of Asian sauces containing chili peppers, vinegar, garlic, sugar, and salt. The sauce may be used as a condiment to accompany meats, poultry, or fish, or it may be included as an ingredient in a dish. When sweet chili sauce is unavailable, make it at home by mixing 1 tablespoon each of corn syrup and rice vinegar with 1 to 2 teaspoons of crushed hot red-pepper flakes.

**Tarragon:** a strong herb with a sweet anise taste. In combination with other herbs—especially rosemary, sage, or thyme—it should be used sparingly, to avoid a clash of flavors. Because heat intensifies tarragon's flavor, cooked dishes require smaller amounts.

**Tofu** (also called bean curd): a dense, unfermented soybean product with a mild flavor. It is rich in protein, relatively low in calories, and free of cholesterol. It is highly perishable and should be kept refrigerated, submerged in water; if the water is changed daily, the tofu may be stored for up to a week.

**Turmeric:** a spice used as a coloring agent and occasionally as a substitute for saffron. It has a musty odor and a slightly bitter flavor.

**Udon:** a fine, flat Japanese wheat noodle.

**Virgin olive oil:** see Olive oil.

**Wheat berries:** unpolished, whole-wheat kernels with a nutty taste and a chewy texture.

**Wild rice:** the seed of a water grass native to the Great Lakes region of North America. Wild rice is appreciated for its robust flavor.

**Zest:** the flavorful outermost layer of citrus-fruit peel; it should be cut or grated free of the white pith that lies just beneath it.

## *Picture Credits*

# Acknowledgments

The editors are particularly indebted to the following people for creating recipes for this volume: Melanie Barnard, New Canaan, Ct.; Peter Brett, Washington, D.C.; Nora Carey, Paris; Robert Chambers, New York; Brooke Dojny, Westport, Ct.; Marie Lou, Bethesda, Md.; Jenni Wright, London.

The editors also wish to thank: Moira Banks, London; Alison Birch, London; Mary Jane Blandford, Alexandria, Va.; Joe Booker, Zamoiski Co., Baltimore, Md.; Jo Calabrese, Royal Worcester Spode Inc., New York; Alexandra Carlier, London; Jackie Chalkley, Washington, D.C.; La

Cuisine, Alexandria, Va.; Jeanne Dale, The Pilgrim Glass Corp., New York; Rex Downey, Oxon Hill, Md.; Flowers Unique, Alexandria, Va.; Dennis Garrett and Ed Nash, The American Hand Plus, Washington, D.C.; Judith Goodkind, Alexandria, Va.; Carol Gvozdich, Alexandria, Va.; Chong Su Han, Alexandria, Va.; Jane Hawker, London; Elizabeth Hodgson, London; Kitchen Bazaar, Washington, D.C.; KitchenAid, Inc., Troy, Ohio; Rebecca Johns, Alexandria, Va.; Gary Latzman and Kirk Phillips, Retroneu, New York; Nancy Lendved, Alexandria, Va.; Leon Stanley, Evan and Mark Lobel, New York; Magruder's, Inc., Rockville, Md.; Nambé Mills Inc., Sante Fe, N.M.; Robin

Olsen, London; Oster, Milwaukee, Wis.; Lisa Ownby, Alexandria, Va.; Prabhu Ponkshe, American Heart Association, Washington, D.C.; C. Kyle and Ruth Randall, Alexandria, Va.; Linda Robertson, JUD Tile, Vienna, Va.; Schiller & Asmus, Inc., Yemasse, S.C.; Jeanette Smyth, Alexandria, Va.; Straight from the Crate, Inc., Alexandria, Va.; Anne Steiner, Alexandria, Va.; Paula Sussman, Alexandria, Va.; Ann Vaughan, Jenn-Air Company, Indianapolis, Ind.; Rita Walters, London; Sarah Wiley, London; Williams-Sonoma, Inc., Alexandria, Va., and Washington, D.C.; CiCi Williamson, Alexandria, Va.; Lynn Addison Yorke, Cheverly, Md.

# Index